THE ORIGIN AND EVOLUTION OF FREEMASONRY CONNECTED WITH THE ORIGIN AND EVOLUTION OF THE HUMAN RACE

By ALBERT CHURCHWARD

M.D., M.R.C.P., F.G.S., P.M., P.Z., 30°

Published 2000
The Book Tree
Escondido, CA

LONDON: GEORGE ALLEN & UNWIN LTD.
RUSKIN HOUSE, 40 MUSEUM STREET, W.C. 1

First published . October 1920
Reprinted . . . October 1921

The Origin and Evolution of Freemasonry
ISBN 978-1-58509-571-1

Published by
The Book Tree
Post Office Box 724
Escondido, CA 92033

TO ALL

MY BROTHER FREEMASONS

THROUGHOUT THE WORLD

WHO ARE SEEKING FOR

THE TRUTH

FOREWARD

The works of Albert Churchward have become classics, and this is no exception. The depth of research is impressive—it goes far beyond the realm of Freemasonry, so it is not necessary to be a Mason to appreciate this book. The origin and evolution of the human race is covered extremely well and takes up almost the entire book. At the same time, Masons will enjoy its somewhat biased stance; for example, Churchward states his belief that the only thing that will save this world from Socialism and anarchy is Freemasonry. The last chapter is a noble call for all Freemasons around the world to engage in making the world a better place to live and to create world peace. It is a political ending to an otherwise mythological and religious research book, but it all fits together quite well.

In fact, the first two chapters are more scientific than anything else, covering atomic structure, electrical forces, and the composition of life itself. Next comes an examination of primitive religious customs and how they became more sophisticated over time. This entire middle area of the book is filled with interesting material. Particularly informative are the areas on the stellar, solar, and lunar cults, the "greater mysteries," and the Egyptian god Horus.

Yes, Churchward has an agenda here. It seems positive, but has not caused me to drop everything and sign up at a Masonic Lodge. (Nothing personal, I just avoid membership to anything.) Yet this is clearly one of the most important and inspiring books that any Freemason could read. It is and has always been known to be one of the most sought after and studied books by those in the Lodge. Making it more accessible in this new edition will hopefully add to the education of many people—people who have high aspirations in life and want to contribute positive and meaningful things to the world. Aside from its potential inspiration, this is a great book to have simply for its interesting collection of facts and theories of life.

Paul Tice

INTRODUCTION

At the present time many countries are suffering from Socialism and Anarchy, with the attendant evils that always have been associated with every nation wherever the ignorant classes have been allowed to predominate in the councils and the government of the country, with the result that civilization has not been retarded only, but set back again for hundreds of years, at least in the progress of evolution in these countries. This evil is now threatening the whole of humanity and can be arrested *permanently* only by the Unity of the Brotherhood of Freemasonry; and it is to point out these facts and the remedy that it has been willed I should write this book for the knowledge of the Brotherhood. The Unity of all the Brotherhood of Freemasonry throughout the world is the only means for a permanent Universal Peace. And what reasons are there against a Universal Brotherhood being formed to establish permanent Peace throughout the world under the principles and tenets of the Craft? Herein have I set forth details of the same.

It is at the request of many Brothers I publish this book. I do so more readily because it supplies a link missing in my former publications, giving to the Brotherhood a further proof of that knowledge which they seek, and which very few, if any, members of the Craft have ever devoted such time and study in scientific research as is necessary to speak with authority on the subject matter.

In order to gain a true conception of the origin and evolution of Freemasonry, its Signs, Symbols, and all its Rituals and Ceremonies, one must have also a knowledge of the origin and evolution of the Human Race, with all the Totemic Mysteries performed in Sign Language by Primitive Man. They are linked together *pari passu*, and the answer as to the origin of all our Brotherhood can be found only by unravelling the mystery and causes as to why we find different Types of the Human Race, their different beliefs being in many cases analogous, and all using the same Signs and Symbols—although under different terminology, and scattered over the face of earth and water throughout this world.

There are two important subjects we must study and master before we can arrive at the critical truth.

The first is the Periodic Laws of the Corpuscles, which govern the evolution and devolution of the Universe and by which T.G.A.O.T.U. created all things, and is for ever creating, and balances devolution by evolution.

The second is the learning and comprehending

"Sign Language" in all its phases, that being the mode of registering the prehistoric past before verbal language came into being, by a continual repetition in the Totemic and other Mysteries or Ceremonies of Primitive Man.

I therefore will try to teach you some knowledge of the Periodic Laws of the Corpuscles—in other words, "The Divine Laws of the Universe"; otherwise you will fail to understand how and why progressive evolution is constantly and for ever taking place, its objective being to a "higher type of Homo"; devolution being but one phase of this progressive evolution.

All the facts I have herein set forth can be verified as the truth by any Brother who will devote sufficient study and scientific research to the subject matter.

These can be found written on stones, papyri, in the *Ritual of the Resurrection* of Ancient Egypt (written in Sign Language), and amongst the inner African and other native tribes in various parts of the world, and follow the Laws of Evolution and the migrations of the Human Race.

I am greatly indebted to the Rev. J. M. Douglas Thomas, F.R.G.S., and Mrs. K. Watkins for correcting the MS. and for the drawings contained in this work.

A. C.

Royal Societies Club,
63 St. James' Street, London,

In publishing the second edition of the *Origin and Evolution of Freemasonry connected with the Origin and Evolution of the Human Race* I have not altered, or added to, the text, but would wish to draw the attention of all the Brotherhood to the *Origin and Evolution of the Human Race* which has now been published, and in which the evolution of the Human Race has been fully exemplified, and will prove to the Brotherhood the critical contents of my works.

A. C.

September 1921.

BY THE SAME AUTHOR

ORIGIN AND ANTIQUITY OF FREEMASONRY

ARCANA OF FREEMASONRY

ORIGIN AND EVOLUTION OF PRIMITIVE MAN

SIGNS AND SYMBOLS OF PRIMORDIAL MAN (1st and 2nd Editions)

ORIGIN AND EVOLUTION OF THE HUMAN RACE

ORIGIN AND EVOLUTION OF RELIGION (*In the press*)

CONTENTS

CONTENTS

ILLUSTRATIONS

ILLUSTRATIONS

The Origin and Evolution of Freemasonry

CHAPTER I

PERIODIC LAWS OF THE CORPUSCLES AND SOCIALISTS

RECENTLY Ethics has been preached and written by men who have not the slightest idea of the harm they are doing to their fellow-creatures and their country. They cannot have any real knowledge of the past history and evolution of the human race, or the causes of the rise and fall of all great nations of the past, or from whence originated the doctrines they believe in, or profess to believe in; also many fallacies are still written and preached by some of our professors and great divines as truths, whereas the truth is entirely different. I therefore hope that this may awaken and teach them before it is too late, and that the human race may not be sent back to the dark and degenerate age from which we have just emerged.

One only has to think and understand that the pursuit and acquisition of truth is of infinite concernment to mankind in the study of the evolution of the human race, and the origin and beliefs and meaning of all the doctrines found throughout the world. By the cultivation of our reason we are better enabled to distinguish good from evil, as well as truth from falsehood; both these are matters of the highest importance, whether we regard this life or the life to come.

A great error is often committed on account of the disguise and false colours in which many things appear when presented to us in an imperfect state. I have seen thousands of things which are not in reality what they appear to be, and that, both in the moral and natural world:

Knavery puts on the face of justice.

Hypocrisy and superstition wear the vizard of piety.

Deceit and evil are often clothed in the shapes and appearances of truth and goodness.

We are imposed upon at home as well as abroad; often deceived in our senses, by our imaginations, by our passions and appetites, by the authority of men, by education and custom: also led into errors by judging according to these false and flattering principles for the want of mature judgment, rather than according to the nature of things and experience of the past, which is true knowledge.

Reason is the glory of human nature and one of the chief eminences whereon we are raised above our fellow-creatures in the lower world.

It is only by reasoning from past experiences and understanding the Periodic Laws that a country or a nation can save itself from downfall and destruction and advance to a higher state of evolution; without this knowledge the humans will not advance much further to a higher type of man than the present highest Homo. But by understanding and following these Laws, humanity may attain a much higher type than it has hitherto reached, and it is for our Brotherhood throughout the world to assist and carry forward this great work.

That my readers may better understand the subject of the Periodic Law,[1] the result of different groupings and the causes for changes in these groupings of Corpuscles, I will give a short description of how this is brought about by portraying it in tabular form, but must first premise for their information that a Corpuscle is a negative particle of electricity which can exist alone, $\frac{1}{1000}$ the size and weight of an Atom of Hydrogen, with a velocity of about 100,000 miles per second, and can penetrate through the thickest block of steel. An Atom is made up of two or more Corpuscles surrounded by Positive Electricity.

[1] I am indebted to Professors J. J. Thomson and R. R. Dunkan for much information on this subject.

Positive Electricity cannot exist alone. Matter is a group of Atoms, either inorganic or organic. With regard to the number and arrangement of Corpuscles, their structure as found in the formation of Atoms, and the different properties that a given structure would confer upon an Atom, they follow the same Periodic Law as for the Elements. If there are two Corpuscles only—1 and 2—they will be in equilibrium if placed on opposite sides of the centre of a sphere:

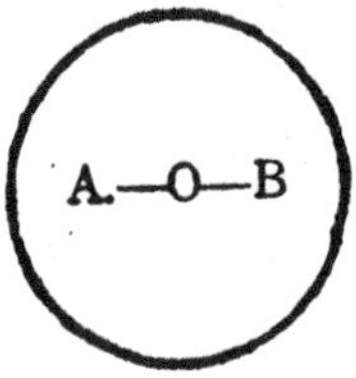

If there are three Corpuscles—1, 2, 3—they will be in equilibrium if they form an equilateral triangle with its centre at the centre of the sphere.

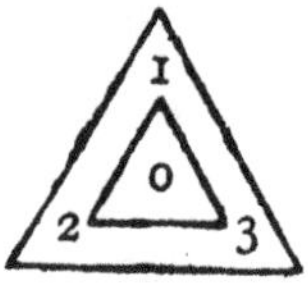

Four Corpuscles will arrange themselves at the corners of a square—

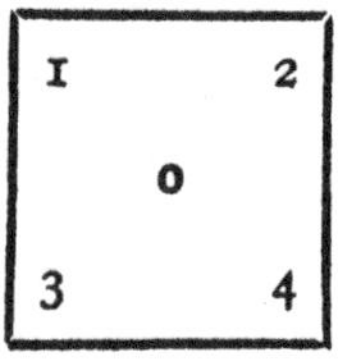

When these Corpuscles exceed five, they break up into two groups.

The group containing the smaller occupies the surface of an inner shell towards the centre. The others are on an outer shell concentric with the inner one, the sphere of Positive Electrification surrounding and balancing them all.

As the number of Corpuscles still further increases, there arrives a stage at which the equilibrium cannot be stable, even with two groups, and the Corpuscles divide themselves into three groups, on three concentric shells; and as numbers further increase, more and more groups are necessary for equilibrium.

For example, the following table will show how the Corpuscles group themselves.

Number of Corpuscles.

15	20	25	30	35	40	45	50	55	60

Number in Successive Rings.

10	12	13	15	16	16	17	18	19	20
5	7	9	10	12	13	14	15	16	16
	1	3	5	6	8	10	11	12	13
				1	3	4	5	7	8
							1	1	3

For further demonstration we must now take an entire series of arrangements with a collection of corpuscles of which the *outer* ring consists of the same definite number—say 20.

Number of Corpuscles.

59	60	61	62	63	64	65	66	67

Number in Successive Rings.

20	20	20	20	20	20	20	20	20
16	16	16	17	17	17	17	17	17
13	13	13	13	13	13	14	14	15
8	8	9	9	10	10	10	10	10
2	3	3	3	3	4	4	5	5

Fifty-nine is the smallest number, 67 is the largest number of Corpuscles in one collection that can have an outer ring of 20.

The mass of the Atom must be the sum of the masses of the Corpuscles it contains, so that the atomic weight is a measure of the number of Corpuscles in the Atom, and—

The properties of an Element are a periodic function of its atomic weight.

It is the same with these corpuscles—in fact, the Elements are a combination of groups of corpuscles.

If, for example, certain properties are connected with a group of 5 corpuscles, these properties will appear again when the number increases to 15; for 15 corpuscles consist of the same group of 5, with 10 others surrounding it.

The properties connected with these two groups of 5 and 15 corpuscles will then disappear, until we again find two groups of 5 and 10 corpuscles respectively, with still another ring surrounding them: this occurs when the corpuscles number

30, when we have a group of 5 surrounded by 10, surrounded by 15, and so on. It means, simply, the periodic recurrence of certain groups of corpuscles as the number of corpuscles constituting the atom increases. We see in this way that we can divide the various groups of corpuscles into families—*each member of the family is derived from the preceding member* and has certain similar definite properties. Now, when any ring is subject to an external disturbance, one or more corpuscles may easily be detached from it. The negative electricity of the collection of corpuscles is just balanced by the sphere of positive electricity surrounding and enclosing it—if, therefore, one negative corpuscle is lost, the whole arrangement will assume a positive change. Such an atom would then behave like the atom of a strongly electro-positive or basic element. Applied to humans, the will, mind or action of an individual would become positive or of an optimistic character. In the case of 59 corpuscles, the number of corpuscles inside is only just sufficient to make the outer ring of 20 stable; this ring will be, therefore, on the verge of instability, and when its corpuscles are displaced the force urging them back again will be small. With the next group, 60 corpuscles, the outer ring is more stable, because there is an additional corpuscle inside it. While it may lose a corpuscle it will not do so as readily as the group 59. Hence, it will not so easily assume the positive charge of electricity, and, therefore, will not be so electro-positive an element as group 59. In the human, the individual will not be so positive in his opinions or force of arguments. Sixty-one corpuscles will be still less electro-positive. When the total number of corpuscles increases, say, up to 63 or 64, the possibility of losing a corpuscle from the outer ring vanishes. When the stability of the atom becomes extreme, one or more corpuscles of the outer ring may actually lie on the surface of the atom without breaking the ring. In this case the atom receives a charge of negative electricity, and would behave like the atom of an electro-negative element. In man, the thoughts, actions and opinions of the individual must assume, therefore, a negative character. This increase in the stability of the ring, and consequently in the electro-negative character of its atom, would augment until it had as many as 67 corpuscles, when the stability of the ring arrives at its maximum ; 67 corpuscles, therefore, consequently represent a strongly electro-negative element, or in the human a *pessimistic character.* Thus we see that, in losing or gaining a corpuscle at the terminal ends in a definite group, changes entirely opposite are brought about, either electro-positive or electro-negative. In the human it would produce *an optimistic or pessimistic character,* or the action of the individual would become active or passive, whilst the corpuscles of the centre of the group are neither electro-positive nor electro-negative and are incapable of receiving any charge of electricity whatever. In the human this is depicted by senile dementia, or the loss of recollection and thought. The atom would not be electro-positive or electro-negative, and as the brain cells are made up of atoms composed of these corpuscles in various groups, almost in pure form, it is easy now to understand why causes such as shell shock, railway accidents, mental shock of any kind, or the bombardment of these corpuscles by others from an outside influence, will convert a normal brain into an abnormal one. Also how the Divine Creator, by increasing the number of groups of these corpuscles, has produced the higher types of Man and higher evolution of the human race. One also obtains the physiological causes for good and evil to which the human race is subject, produced by evil or good influences outside the individual, or individuals, acting on the various groups of corpuscles in the brain cells of the objective, causing one group of corpuscles to lose a corpuscle at one of its terminals and another to gain it, by this arrangement possessing different properties. This occurs by what is called valency (grabbing power). A univalent positive series is one which, under certain circumstances, attains stability by *losing one corpuscle.* A univalent negative series is one that will *acquire one*, and one only, of the corpuscles of another series.

A divalent positive series is one which will *lose two corpuscles* and no more, and a divalent negative series will *acquire two* or more.

The valency of the series is thus simply a question of the number of corpuscles that can escape from, or be received by, the corpuscular groupings which constitute any kind of series. We here perceive how impressionable brains or an unstable condition of the groups of corpuscles are easily acted upon by outside influences, or by those corpuscles which are grouped and possess strongly positive or negative conditions. I give one group as an example only to demonstrate to my readers how changes take place by the subtraction or addition to one or more corpuscles from the group, proving how a positive can be converted into a negative or vice versa; whether it be actions, thoughts or elements, either in inorganic or organic matter, the results are always similar. For instance, we will take the inorganic element Hydrogen, an atom of which possesses 1,000 corpuscles=H, and Oxygen=O, which has 16,000 corpuscles to make up one atom.

Now, when these atoms combine under certain conditions an interchange takes place in their groupings, and what is called a chemical compound is the result. Two atoms of Hydrogen grab one of Oxygen, or one atom of Oxygen grabs two of Hydrogen, and the oxide of Hydrogen, i.e., water, is formed = H_2O.

In the inorganic world, or in the elements, the groupings and number of corpuscles are the simplest: in the vegetable world a greater evolution takes place and the groupings are more complex; when we come to the animal world there are still greater numbers of groupings and still more complexity; in the highest type of the human race they are the greatest. In much of the inorganic world, radio-active matter is constantly returning these corpuscles to their original form. This inorganic world has been formed by the simple process of lowering the temperature from 30,000° Cent., when all were corpuscles only, and as the temperature cooled, so the various elements were formed at different degrees of temperature, by different groupings: ultimately all will revert to simple corpuscles again—because the Sun, the centre of our system of all the planets that have been thrown off from it, is cooling down, and in time, how long it is impossible to say, will become cold and dead; then these will clash together again with others that have arrived at the same condition, the constant bombardment and clashing together, each one being attracted to the centre of the swarm, causing intense heat; so that ultimately a temperature of about 30,000° Cent. will be produced, with the result that all the elements and matter split up into the original corpuscles from which they were formed and a new star comes into existence. We can see and prove by the telescope and spectroscope the changes as they take place; also, as the star cools down again, we can see how the elements are re-formed at the various temperatures that occur in the process. This proves that evolution and devolution in the Universe are balanced and that nothing is lost: only a transference and a transformation takes place of energy and matter.

It is the same in the organic as in the inorganic world: given a person's mind or thoughts in a stable condition upon any particular or definite subject, his brain cells are made up of these groups of corpuscles just on the balance of stability, i.e. on the line or condition of a series that is in a stable condition—electrically—a normal brain. But something occurs outside his brain cells which affects this series, say shock or acute mental emotion, or only a bombardment of this series of corpuscles by others outside, for example; first it alters the grouping of this series and the result is a change from the previous mental condition, which has been a normal one, but now becomes either a positive or negative state of abnormal action or thought; in certain events it might render the grouping of the corpuscles into that state which is neither positive nor negative, and these groupings are incapable of receiving or losing another corpuscle—his mind or brain then would become "lost," i.e. he would be quite incapable of thought or impressions—"His mind is a blank."

The evolution of the organic follows the same law, or rather is a continuance of the same laws of the inorganic. As I stated *supra*, in the lower forms of life the composition and groupings of these corpuscles are comparatively few and simple. The human follows on under the same law—take, for example, the lowest Homo, the brain of a Pygmy—Primitive Man. Here we find what is called the grey matter, from which all thoughts, will and ideas emanate, comparatively thin, and the sulci of the brain are not deep. In the highest type of man this grey matter is the thickest and the brain has the deepest sulci. In the different types between the highest and lowest we find many variations, the grey matter always getting thicker and the sulci deeper as we advance in the upward trend of evolution.

Evolution being ever progressive, so these corpuscles ever multiply in numbers and series, and this is always the case normally. But if from any cause or causes this progress is interrupted, then the negative which will constitute a degenerative form will predominate, and a retrograde action may be the result.

This is briefly the Periodic Law, or God's Law, or as it is commonly called the Law of Nature, which few people study and fewer comprehend.

Yet these Laws are true and immutable. In

them we possess the key to gain the whole knowledge of the secrets of the Universe, Life and Death and the Hereafter; the causes and effects of the rise and fall of all nations—for the causes and the results we see developed in the human for good or ill; the actions, thoughts, the different attitudes assumed by men and women, who may live under the same surroundings, but who in thoughts, actions, and words are diametrically opposed to each other in their opinions on any given subject, each one supposing and believing himself to be right, yet at the same time many labouring under the greatest fallacy, because the normal condition of the corpuscles of the atoms comprising their brain cells has received wrong impressions, either positive or negative, the result of different groupings. This may occur in many ways, i.e. by reading that which is not true, being erroneously taught, or having their brain corpuscles bombarded by others outside, by suggestion, or any other pernicious influence. Disease will also produce the same results, or, if I may put it in another way, some of these causes will produce disease, which is a disarrangement of the corpuscles of one or more series. In some cases where (too many of) the brain corpuscles have not escaped to any great extent from the one normal series, by treatment, this may recover again the corpuscles which have escaped, and so we have then a return of a normal brain. As an example, a man with a normal brain holds a certain and definite opinion on a given subject: some one has impressed him, say by talking to him, or he may have an objective shock in some form, which causes him to change that previous and true opinion into one which is false; later he may, by physical or some other evidence impressing a positive or negative action on the corpuscles, find that his first opinion was correct, and so will think again rightly—normally. Here a corpuscle has escaped from one series and joined another, but its electrical attachment or attraction to its last series is not great, and so it may easily detach itself and rejoin its original series or group. The foregoing will fully explain to the Physiologist the curious pathological conditions which have recently been developed, probably for the first time in the human, causing the abnormal symptoms which we term "shell shock."

The cause of some diseases is that the normal groupings of the corpuscles of the cells of certain tissues or of the blood have from some cause or another undergone different groupings, and the tissue and blood become abnormal; now, treatment will *rectify this*. For example, we want the blood more acid: aluminium hydroxide in this case will be effective, because it increases the hydrogen ion concentration, and when absorbed the metallic ion (Al) takes up three hydroxyl (OH) molecules, being *trivalent*, and this leaves an excess of Hydrogen (H) ions. On the other hand, salicic acid makes the blood more basic, because the silicon ion has the opposite charge to alumen, and so by this means the corpuscles regain their original groupings in the atoms forming the tissues involved; the disease thus becomes eliminated and the patient cured. There is so much to be learnt on this subject that I look forward to see such a great advance made in the future medical treatment on these lines as will astonish the world and bring a great deal of human suffering to an end, but it is not a subject to dilate on here. There is no spontaneity in nature or the laws of nature that can be demonstrated by scientific research. The universe is harmonious, composed of three physical entities, Matter, Ether, and Energy. These three phases, although appearing to be separate and distinct, are in reality one. They are forms or phases of a reality, bound together by the Divine God to form His Universe, and, if I may express it, "His Laws of Nature," and you cannot create or destroy an atom or corpuscle of the same, neither can you arrest the devolution and evolution which is constantly taking place. Is the poetry of nature destroyed when one knows these laws? In my opinion it is a thousand times increased, and the wisdom of man is but foolish in comparison. We know and must believe in these days, because we can prove it by scientific experiments, that everything in

God's Universe of World and Stars is made up of corpuscles, the ultimate constituent part of the atoms of all the elements as known to chemists. Men and women, mice and elephants, the belts of Jupiter and the rings of Saturn, every mechanical work of earth, air, fire and water, every criminal act, every human deed of love or valour—all are made up of these corpuscles and the relation of one swarm of corpuscles to another. Here, for example, is a swarm of corpuscles vibrating, scintillant, martial—they call it a soldier; and anon in France or Germany that swarm dissolves —dissolves, forsooth, because of another little swarm they call shells. What a phantasmagoric dance it is, these corpuscles of atoms! Mark you the mutabilities of things. These same corpuscles, or others like them, come together again, vibrating, clustering, interlocking, combining, and the result is a woman, a flower, a blackbird or shark, as the case may be. But to-morrow the dance is ended and the corpuscles and atoms are far away—some in fever germs that broke up the dance; others are the green hair of the grave, and others are blown about the antipodes on the waves of the ocean, and the eternal ever-changing dance goes on.

One thing, therefore, is sure: that every action of everything living or dead, within the bourne of time and space, is the action of one swarm of corpuscles on another, for without them there is but empty void. These are God's little servants which nothing can destroy. You take a piece of coal, composed of these corpuscles and atoms; you burn it, and you can convert this consecutively into heat, into mechanical energy, into electrical energy, and in some far away street into the radiant energy of the arc-lamp. Or take a piece of iron and heat it to 30,000° Cent.; presto! these little corpuscles fly off and unite with others —the moist atmosphere—and form clouds, descending again as rain to form rivers and oceans. Again "the dead stars" clash together, and the result an ever-increasing temperature, until it has reached a degree of 30,000° Cent., and lo! a new star, a new world is formed, and at that temperature all are in the form of our little corpuscles; these gradually cool down again until the chemical elements of which this world is composed are found. This evolution and devolution is repeated and repeated, but God's little servants are never destroyed, not one; they only assume other forms of swarms, or they can exist by themselves, and then so small, $\frac{1}{1000}$ the size of an atom of hydrogen. And how fast they can travel—90,000 to 100,000 miles per second—and what can stop them? Nothing, for they can penetrate the biggest block of steel; and with these little atoms God has created all and everything, and is for ever creating.

There is no spontaneity in the creations; all

are governed by a well-known law—the Periodic Law. These corpuscles, when *existing alone*, possess the same properties, and when combined, always in definite combinations, each possesses definite properties which never exist precisely the same in any other combination. If a different quantity of these unite, or combine, a different property is evolved. These form the Alphabet of all things living or dead.

The Socialists state that "Nature is not like the products or works of man"—no; because man could never produce that which God can with His little servants. All man can do is to use these, mechanically or otherwise, and produce different forms of things, either material or diverse, such as good or bad actions or thoughts. He cannot, however, produce the ultimate forms of the very atoms with which he works. These are given to him by a Divine Creator in order to attain a higher type, a higher standard, for himself and those who follow him. As man has advanced up the ladder of evolution, so by the Divine Will these corpuscles have with Time produced a higher type of the human from the original, by different combinations of the corpuscles forming the brain cells, and the law of evolution is tending to be always progressive and to evolve a superior Homo. When men or nations do not follow the laws of evolution, one little swarm of the brain cells will convert another little swarm into a third form, and those men or nations will eventually become destroyed, and these corpuscles will unite again somewhere to form a higher type in other men or nations, for the progressive evolution which is constantly taking place. How could these things be if there was no Great Divine Creator? It is the eternal law of evolution, *the key* to learn. This knowledge lies in the Periodic Law of the corpuscles and elements. Here only can you find your Alphabet, learn to spell and then read the Universe of God—not the Socialist's Universe. They contend that if the individual is a complete and independent totality, if his end be in himself, then any voluntary self-restraint, let alone self-sacrifice, on the part of the individual is unintelligible. If the individual contains his end within himself as person, where can the obligation lie to prefer a painful course which can never possibly redound to the ulterior interest? *He recognizes the call to do and to forbear only in things which directly affect the society,* all actions not having a direct social bearing being morally indifferent to him. In this conception of duty, the individual consciously subordinates himself to the community, not limited by frontier, but world embracing. Thus we shall see later in this book that the only difference between the Aboriginal Tribes and the present-day Socialists is, that the Aboriginal Tribes' first and only Tribal Ethic was for the Tribes or Totemic Clan alone into which the aboriginal was born, or belonged, but he believed in a Supreme Being and a life hereafter. In the case of the Socialists it embraces, or would do so, all the Tribes of the world, but with no belief in a Supreme Being or a life hereafter. In Socialism, Ethics becomes political, and Politics become Ethical, whilst Religion in the end is consigned to be absorbed in a corporate social consciousness of which the *telos* is the final purpose of Society, thus implying that there is no life hereafter or spiritual second life.

That is a great fallacy and the cause of unbelief in the phenomena of Spirit Life hereafter. There is one man I am glad to see who writes with the courage of his convictions—Sir Oliver Lodge, F.R.S. Although he has *some proof* of the borderland and the beyond, he is far from knowing the whole truth, nor does he yet possess the key to gain the entrance to the secrets of the future life. In his various works, to one who knows and possesses the key, this is evident. His article " Must Nature Perish ? " I answered in the *Freemason*, April 22, 1916. His recent articles in the *Daily Chronicle* and in his book on *Raymond, or Life and Death*, prove to me beyond a doubt that he has not been using a *good* spiritual medium—these are very few and rare to find, but many exist. He would not have written *Life and Death*, and expressed his experiences in the terminology that he has, if his medium had been a *good spirit*, and this I challenge to prove to him objectively if he so desires. Much that he has written, however, is absolutely true. He states: "A chief obstacle in the way of recognizing the possibility of survival of bodily death is the fact that loss of body means the loss of brain, and that so the mind appears to cease to work. At any rate, the brain ceases to work; and the question arises, how then can memory persist? If memory is located in the brain and nowhere else, memory cannot survive the destruction of that organ. But if survival of memory is proved experimentally, we can take it as demonstrated that memory is not, or not solely, located in the brain." His answer to his own question is bad logic, because if the brain perishes so do all other parts of the body; he is at fault because he does not understand or know the truth. If all perishes nothing can remain, yet he knows memory does remain. I answer, the truth is that memory *is located in the brain corpuscles, and in the brain corpuscles alone.* And although the matter part dies the corpuscles do not die, but still exist, and can be seen, the same as the body corpuscles. *The whole spirit of the man or woman after death has no material body or material brain,* but these exist *as the likeness of the body and brain in a bright corpuscular form.* The Periodic Law provides for this. Many after death do not remember anything of this life here on earth until it is recalled to them. The brain may be compared to a book with many blank leaves, and each day you print or write a page in this book during your life on earth. How many people can tell you all they have printed in this book? If asked about a certain thing that has happened, they say they have forgotten—*their memory fails them*; and yet an hour or so after they remember all about it, by some incident perhaps that has been brought to their notice. It has been photographed on the corpuscles all the time, but they have not been able to turn to the right page of the book. And so it is after death; at a certain time all is recalled to them. In no part of the body have you matter which possesses the same physiological effect as the brain. Here you have the brain tissue composed of corpuscles and ions almost in their pure form embodied in so-called matter, and it is owing to the disarrangement of these corpuscles and ions from their normal conditions that men's minds and memories become abnormal. It is by the knowledge of how to use these corpuscles that the mind, or will, of one who knows can operate upon another body submitted to its temporary guidance and control, also how to re-form these corpuscles in their normal and original groups which constitute what is termed a normal brain. (In shell shock and injuries to the brain by any concussion, such as railway accidents, etc., these corpuscles are disorganized from their normal group constitutions; in other words, by the injury received they have regrouped themselves under the Periodic Law into groups and forms which possess different properties from the original.)

Sir Oliver Lodge states: "However it be accomplished, and whatever reception the present-day scientific world may give to the assertion, there are many now who know, by first-hand experience, that communication is possible across the boundary —if there is a boundary between the world apprehended by our few animal-derived senses and the larger existence concerning which our knowledge is still more limited; communication is not easy, but it occurs." Let me assure him that to those who possess the secret and know, as the old Wise Men of Egypt knew, it is quite easy if you understand the Periodic Law of the Corpuscles.

If you wish to know the truth you can only work with good mediums, and you must never use bad spiritual mediums. You ask, How do you know, or how can you distinguish the one from the other? The answer is that it is quite easily done when you possess the secret knowledge of how to send them to the Gates of Paradise and pass them through the Maa-Kheru of the Ancient Egyptian High Priests. The knowledge of the Periodic Law of the Corpuscles gives you the key to unlock the book containing the hidden mysteries of the Universe. It points out to you clearly and definitely the causes of the fall of every great nation.

In the course of time, Science, which now rightly demands verification and proof, will discover the secret and acknowledge the truth. But scientists as a whole have much to learn, and until they take the trouble to do so they will not make any great advancement or gain any real knowledge regarding the secrets of nature and the cosmic laws.

I have been induced to make these statements because I know that I know, and because Sir Oliver Lodge in his *Life and Matter*, p. 58, writes on this subject as follows: "And those who think they have such a contribution to make, and such a revelation entrusted to them, are bound to express it to the best of their ability, and leave it to their contemporaries and successors to assimilate such portions of it as are true and to develop it further." Although I have known some of the secrets of the old Egyptian Urshi for many years, and proved them to be true, I have not written these truths before. All those who are interested in the Laws of the Spiritual World must, therefore, thank Sir Oliver Lodge for my setting these forth in this book. I can only add that I quite agree with Sir Oliver in his criticism of Professor Häckel's writings—only more so.

Herbert Spencer could find no origin for the idea of an after-life save the conclusion which the savage draws from the notion suggested by dreams (Spencer, *Facts and Comments*, p. 210).

But whatsoever dreams the savage had, they would become familiar in the course of time. He would learn that dreams had no power to externalize themselves in apparitions, had there been no ghosts or visible spirits of the dead. He would also learn readily enough, and the lesson would be perpetually repeated, that howsoever great his success when hunting in his dreams of the night, there was no game caught when he awoke in the morning. Clearly no reliance could be placed on dreams for establishing the ghost, any more than on the result of other dreams. Moreover, the same savage who is assumed to have panned out on dreams for a false belief also reports that he sees the spirits of the dead by abnormal vision and has the means of communicating with them. But all the credulity of all the savages who ever existed cannot compete or be compared with the credulity involved in this belief or assumption that the ghost itself, together with the customs, the ceremonies, the religious rites of evocation and propitiation, the priceless offerings, the countless testimonies of the veritability of abnormal vision, the universal practices for inducing that vision for the purpose of communicating with spiritual intelligence, had no other than a subjective basis, and a false belief that the dream-shadow was the sole reality. Can one conceive anything more fatal to this, made on behalf of evolution as a mode of nature's teaching than this assumption that man universally has been the victim of an illusion derived from a baseless delusion? If primitive men were the victims of a delusion which has been continued for thousands of years in defiance of all experience and observation, what guidance or trust could there be in evolution: or how are we to distinguish between the false product and the true if man dreamed the ghost into being when there was no ghost, if he had been so far the victim of his own Frankenstein as to found the whole body of his religious beliefs and customs on that which never existed? Primitive man was not a hundredth part so likely to be the victim of hallucination or diseased subjectivity as the modern. External nature is not hallucinative; it is the scene of continuous education in primal or rudimentary and constantly recurring realities. His elemental spirits or forces were real, and not the result of hallucination; why not his ancestral spirits? African spiritualism, which might be voluminously illustrated, culminated in the Egyptian Mysteries. The Mystery Teachers were so far advanced as phenomenal spiritualists, and say so little about it in any direct manner, that it has taken one who owns to have a profound experience of the phenomena many years to come up with them in studying the eschatology of the *Ritual*.

There are many people in this world who are Spiritualists—scientific men and others, but few possess the true knowledge and secret of action.

The Divine God creates new Stars or new Worlds to serve His purpose and Will; these when their allotted task is finished decay and die out, and then are re-formed into new Stars or Worlds; so it is with man from the lowest Pygmy: each type rises to a higher type, evolution is progressive, and it is only because the great masses of people do not comprehend this and have followed the teachings of ignorant men that Socialism and Bureaucracy have arisen, and consequently caused the destruction of great nations.

The individual is only a partly complete totality in this world, but to a great extent independent, the influence of good spirits and bad spirits being antagonistic; his own consciousness and conceptions being the individual factors to decide the issue, the ultimate decision is often influenced by material circumstances, other swarms of corpuscles in present human craniums bombarding his own. Education to a higher standard is the only means to eradicate these bad influences and impressions, which are thus against his ulterior interests. His complete totality is only achieved in Paradise by the blending of the male and female into one whole. Therefore the fallacy of the Socialistic arguments. The human has passed Totemic Sociology; he is partially an independent totality in himself, but owes a duty to the State or country to which he belongs, and above all has a duty to the Divine Creator, inasmuch that if he does not follow the Divine Laws laid down by evolution he will ultimately become annihilated,[1] both as an earthly human and also a spirit form. He is independent if he does not break the laws of the country; these are laid down in all well organized society for the good and well-being of society: although many of our laws are bad, yet it remains with the majority to rectify them if they will. He is independent to follow the Laws of the Divine Creator; if he obeys, he has his final reward, eternal happiness—not as God Himself or a part of Him, as the Socialists preach it must be, if there is a Divine Creator, but as one of His servants. The result, however, if he does not is total destruction. The Ancient Egyptians knew these secrets, but when their old Wise Men were destroyed the only evidence left was written on stone and papyrus. And this has ever been the case when nations have been laid waste and ruined; their wise men were killed and all art and learning ended, as far as the conquerors were able, and the whole country lapsed into barbarism and decay. But a few escaped to hand down the secrets to posterity when the chosen people should know them again, so lifting the human race to a still higher standard. This time is beginning to dawn

[1] I mean by this the annihilation and destruction of this spiritual body into original corpuscles without groupings.

on humanity, if you stamp out and kill the cancer that is consuming the life of the country; if you do not, darkness and ignorance will still prevail until new men or new nations arise with less narrow-minded and bigoted opinions. The Socialist is far inferior morally to the poor aborigine; he is so imbued with self-interest that to work or act without personal advantage would be to admit the inadequacy of himself as an end in himself. He is so egotistic that he cannot admit there is a Divine Creator Who formed and created an infallible law—the Periodic Law—to govern and carry on the evolution and devolution of the Universe. The Socialist is so conceited that he places his own works and thoughts on a higher plane than any Divine Creator. He states: "Did I become conscious, however dimly, however transiently, of 'myself' as having lived and played a part amid the life of past ages, then I could believe in a continuance in the future, but my personal identity begins with a certain year; beyond that I have no personal identity." He does not consider or understand that except the doctrine of transmigration was true this could not be the case, and inasmuch as this doctrine is a fallacy, founded on the belief that the elemental spirits were living personalities at one time, there could be no knowledge of personal identity, however dim, to remind him of a former life—which did not exist.

The poor aborigines make little spirit-houses, and place food therein to propitiate the spirits of their ancestors, and offer sacrifices to the Great Spirit; they also propitiate the elemental or animistic spirits—but they do not believe that these latter ever possessed any form of humanity; they knew better, and it is through the ignorance of later humans in not understanding this that the doctrine of transmigration of souls arose and came into existence. The above must be sufficient proof, then, that the poor aborigines are morally a higher standard of the human than the Socialists.

The Socialist recognizes a duty, however, to the world-wide society to which he belongs, but to nothing else. His argument is fallacious because ethically there can be no difference if the society is a State, clan, or world-wide—it is a duty to society, to which he belongs. He ignores recognizing a duty to his Divine Creator because he professes not to believe in any, and yet, mark well the consciousness of his brain cells, which inform him that there is; but he gets over this by admitting a "first cause" only. Whatever that may mean to him, he is still in the dark and unable to make further explanation regarding it; he has jumped into a deep pit of mud from which he cannot extricate himself, although he attempts to do so by using metaphysical arguments and Platonic terminology. His "first cause" is the

Periodic Law of the Corpuscles and Elements, which he does not understand. If he could comprehend this, his consciousness would convince him that the final purpose of this immutable law did not end with him personally here, or yet the *telos* of his society itself, but that his birth and life on this earth was only one phase in the evolution of Life Eternal. The whole human life has been from the first, and is still so here, one state of transition to a higher type, interrupted now and again by the downfall of a great nation, which has reached the highest type for the time, the cause being in all cases the introduction of Socialism and Bureaucracy. But gradually the course of evolution continues, carried on by other nations, which arise out of the ashes of the dead. Socialists believe in the physical or materialistic principle of the life of mankind.

If the materialist calls science to his aid, it is only to find that his difficulties increase as his scientific investigation goes on. He is met at the outset with the fact that the purely materialistic hypothesis utterly fails to render any adequate interpretation of the phenomena of life. To the materialist the question "whence I came and whither I go" remains unanswered when you bid him look round the universe and direct his attention in turn to the animal and vegetable kingdom, to the sea, to the stars and different constellations by night, to life and death; and when you ask him what is the meaning of it all, he can only generalize on his unknown laws of nature, and omits to account for the origin and purpose of nature, or the future life which the Spiritualist knows to exist.

The highest ethical code of our Brotherhood embraces all the supreme principles of human intelligence, goodness and righteousness, resistance of evil, love for each other and living for the good of all; it is the supreme witness and exponent of the highest religious doctrine; it holds that these are Divine and supreme eternal laws for individual and social action, which are the principles of the mind and Will of God. They are unalterable and eternally true, and men and nations can only live truly by obeying and *co-operating with* these laws.

CHAPTER II

LIFE AND WHAT IT IS—MATERIAL, SPIRITUAL AND EVOLUTIONAL

AND Life—what is Life? No one has yet learned how it was engendered; why, when, or where, not only in man but in animals and plants.

According to the prevalent conception of life, human life is the short time from the birth to the death of man's animal part. But this is not all that life is in the human; this is merely the existence of man as an animal personality. Human life is certainly something which reveals itself in the animal existence, just as organic life is something which reveals itself in the existence of matter—an unknown combination of series of corpuscles. The animal may live for his own body only; nothing prevents his living thus: he satisfies his individuality and unconsciously plays his part, and does not know that he is an individual; but reasoning man cannot live for his own body alone. He cannot live thus because he knows he is an individual, and, therefore, realizes that other people are individuals also, and understands all that must result from the relations of the one to the other. Man himself makes his real life in this world, and lives it. But in two modes of existence bound up with this life man cannot take part, i.e. his spiritual body and matter constituting him. The former is composed of all pure corpuscles which exist eternally in his bodily form. The latter, of a series of corpuscles forming his component parts; which on death and disintegration assume other series of corpuscles and forms. The study of these forms of existence, included within and constituting him as a whole, i.e. his Spiritual and the Material, constituting the animal, shows man the universal Periodic Laws of all existence. Man does not know, and cannot know, any other life of his former self, scrutinize his past as carefully as he will. If he has learnt the Periodic Laws of the Corpuscles, he knows how he has been formed by various combinations of series of these, but he has no knowledge from whence these were derived, or how formed, or what combinations these assume to form his whole, or what form they will take after the disintegration of his material body.

The Spiritual or higher or better part of man's life—the everlasting Spiritual corpuscular body contained in the material body, is always striving towards the good, happiness and welfare of himself and fellow-men. But the common herd of unthinking men understand the welfare of man to be the welfare of his animal part.

Yet his consciousness or Spiritual Self, which he will discover definitely at some indefinite period during his life, will always call upon and tell him that the true life of love for others is the only one that will confer lasting happiness upon him, and that there is another form of life, after this animal life has been annihilated, that will exist for eternity. The gnosis to obtain this everlasting Spiritual Life, which Ethics was first promulgated by Taht-Aan in *The Ritual of Resurrection* or *The Egyptian Book of Life*, has been carried down through the past ages by the so-called "Speculative Freemasons," time and circumstances being the causes of substituting the innovations in place of those fragments which have been lost or as yet have not been found.

The discovery of the Periodic Laws of the Corpuscles is the discovery of science, and applies equally to the Natural or Physical Laws, the Cosmic Laws and the Laws of the Spiritual World,—one is identically a continuation of the other,—and knowing therefore that these Laws are the Laws of the Spiritual World, that whole region at once falls within the domain of science and secures a basis as well as an illustration in the constitution and course of nature; from the beginning to the end it becomes the discerning faculty, clairvoyant power of seeing the eternal in the temporal. The unity of conception becomes complete. The perfection of unity is attained where there is infinite variety of phenomena, infinite complexity of relation. *All known phenomena can be arranged in one vast circle under the Periodic Laws of the Corpuscles, being caused by the various groupings of the different series of corpuscles, separating and uniting into particular groups*—these being the ultimate atoms that the Universe is built up of, and every expression of thought, word, or deed is caused by various groupings into different numbers of these "little bricks" of the Great Creator.

My own opinion is that life is not dependent upon the bodily matter—that life is an unknown combination of a series of corpuscles, which in the human at least continues to exist for eternity. What is commonly called the "spirit" consists of pure corpuscles in series, in the form of the person which once lived as a human, only much more beautiful. There is not the slightest doubt of this in my mind, because I know two people still living who possess the inestimable gift of seeing and being able to converse or communicate with their friends, who never leave them night or day. But these good spirits cannot talk so that one can hear them; they cannot make noises, nor can you take photographs of them: *all this that Spiritualists tell you is chicanery and humbug.* You cannot take photographs of spirits because they are composed of pure corpuscles—Beta Rays; and as it is the Beta Ray that produces photographs, naturally it cannot produce itself. If you ask them a question, they will make a motion of affirmation or negation only; but if you have a good spiritual medium, whom you send into a hypnotic state, you can converse, gain any information you wish that they are permitted to tell you, and they will answer questions or communicate their wishes. The Ancient Egyptian Priests knew this and gained much knowledge through this means. But the real secrets are known to a few only, and since the fall of the Old Egyptian Empire the ignorance of the human always has been such that great opposition has always been, and still is, shown to the study of the Laws of the Spiritual World. But future generations will become more enlightened, and the knowledge that we shall gain through this means may be the source of enlightening us as to *what life is* and all the secrets of the Universe.

Man has come so far up the ladder of knowledge and evolution that it is unthinkable there is not still a higher state to attain, and that ultimately we shall be able to gain the knowledge which up to the present we have not obtained. It is not likely that the Divine Creator should leave His work unfinished. In the higher degrees we are instructed to become PHILOSOPHERS.

All philosophy is in some sense the endeavour to find a unifying principle, to discover the most general conception underlying the whole field of nature and of knowledge. According to Schopenhauer, "*Will*" is the fundamental reality of the world, the thing itself; and its objectivation is what is presented in phenomena. The struggle of the will to realize itself evolves the organism, which in its turn evolves intelligence as the servant of the will. And in practical life the antagonism between the will and the intellect arises from the fact that the former is the metaphysical substance, the latter something accidental and secondary. But the "*Will*" of Schopenhauer is a swarm of corpuscles acting on another swarm of corpuscles in the atoms and molecules of the brain tissue; some electrical or other cause changes these swarms of corpuscles (which as far as the will is concerned are dormant) into activity, and a *will* to think or do is the result; that is the true science of his philosophy.

"Häckel and his followers maintain that when the material organism decays, the vital energy no longer exists, but is resolved into inorganic energies associated with gases and relics of the decaying body. He states that science always finds these inorganic energies to reappear on the dissolution of life, and has never in a single instance found the slightest reason to suspect that the vital force, as such, has continued to exist."

I do not understand what Häckel means by "vital force," except life, and if that is so he is quite wrong. *First, as Sir Oliver Lodge justly states, life is not a form of energy; it belongs to a separate order of existence,* which interacts with this material frame of things, and whilst in this material body exerts guidance and control on the energy which already exists in the elements which compose the material body. Life does not alter the quantity of energy; it utilizes available energy, the same as living things are able to direct inorganic terrestrial energy along new and special paths, so as to achieve results which without "life" could not have occurred. Life is a guiding principle, a controlling agency; i.e. life does guide and influence the elements of inorganic nature, and when the "body" dies, that simply reverts into the inorganic elements. Life as in the human, at least, still continues to exist; to most people it is by no means alone, i.e. without being incorporated in matter, apprehensible to their senses; but undoubtedly others have an inestimable and unpurchasable gift and are able to see it, and with these it does not depend on matter for its visuality. This proves that it is independent, that its essential existence is continuous and permanent, and its interactions with matter are discontinuous and temporary.

Whether the life of plants and animals is the same is another question upon which I would have some doubt, for the reason that the series of corpuscles composing them have not yet manifested such a complete series as in the human, and as I look upon evolution as a progressive stage,

I can conceive that it is only in the human where life has a persistent and eternal state of combination of these complex series. I conceive it possible that life commenced as a simple living cell made up of a certain and definite combination of corpuscles, which by a process of evolution gradually grew into more complexity until Homo appeared, and that it was not until this stage that a corpuscular form analogous to Homo was formed.

But there is no known proof on this point.

I do not understand what Sir Oliver Lodge means when he states (*Life and Death*, p. 318): "A Power that may properly be called *supernatural*."

Does he mean an elementary power—*superhuman*?

The expression altogether is: "In other words, they have essentially recognized the existence of a Power transcending ordinary nature—a Power that may properly be called *supernatural*."

All the elementary powers are *superhuman*.

The powers possessed by a very few persons, of whom I profess to be one, of being able to communicate with our "Glorious Ancestors" in Paradise, and sometimes even with the Great God Himself, are only human powers, founded on the knowledge of the Periodic Laws of the Corpuscles.

I know of no *supernatural* power.

Amongst all aboriginal races the belief in the

living spirit after the death of the body is universal. That is the religion of all ancient spiritualism distinguished from animism. The spirits of the dead are accepted as operative realities.

The Christian cult is the only one religion in the world that was based upon the corpus instead of the resurrection in spirit. In no other religion is continuity in spirit made dependent on the resurrection of the earthly body. The Christians mistook the risen mummy in Amenta for the corpse that was buried on earth, whereas the Egyptian religion was founded on the rising again of the spirit *from* the corpse, as it was imaged in the resurrection of Amsu-Horus transforming from the mummy Osiris, and by the human soul emerging alive from the body of dead matter. There is no instance recorded, in all the experience of spiritualists, ancient or modern, of the corpse coming back from the tomb. The so-called worship of ancestors depended entirely on the ancestors being considered as living, conscious, acting and recipient spirits, and not as corpses mouldering in the earth. This furnishes the sole *raison d'être* for all the sacrificial offerings, the life, the blood, the food, the choicest and costliest things that could be given to the dead. Those whom we call *dead* were to them the veritable living in superhuman forms possessing superhuman powers. John Tanner bears witness to the reality of being able to see the " spirit body."

He was himself inducted into a state of abnormal seership by the Indian Medamen, and saw a spirit in the shape of a young man, who said to him: "I look down upon you at all times, and it is not necessary you should call me with such loud cries" (*Narration*, p. 189; New York, 1837).

Clairvoyance was "the vision and the faculty divine," the "beatific vision" of all the early races. It was sought for and cultivated, prized and protected, as the most precious of all human gifts, and the possessor was held to be divine—the nearest approach to a human divinity.

Miss Kingsley states: "Every West African tribe has a secret society. Every free man has to pass through the secret society of his tribe. If during this education the elders of the society discover that a boy is what is called in Calabar an Ebumtup—a person who can see spirits—they advise that he should be brought up to the medical profession" (Kingsley, *W.A.S.*, p. 214).

The old Her-Seshta,[1] or Wise Men of Egypt, indicated that man may become co-worker with both nature and Divinity on these higher planes if he will.

He may sit in the Councils of Destiny and help to shape the progress of the race, or he may crawl like a worm and be trodden under foot till, through misery and pain, he struggles to the Light.

[1] There were seven classes with different names of these old Priests of Egypt.

But few that remained of those who were not slaughtered in past ages were duly and truly worthy and qualified ; but these few have preserved the message which they have transmitted unimpaired through ages, that will some day make man free and develop in an equal degree his spiritual faculties as compared with his physical power.

Equity along the line of justice and right will lay the foundation for a grander civilization that will secure social order, because it must be an organization of individuals actuated by a desire to do right under the light formulated by untrammelled reason and conscience ; thus shall justice be universal and want and misery unknown.

So many great errors and evils have arisen from bad observation and reasoning that it becomes a natural question to ask how it comes to pass that man observes and reasons so badly, when his business is to observe and reason. Because he is a limited being, with very limited capacity, while that which he has to observe and reason about is illimitable. Observation is a process of mental growth, slow and tedious necessarily, and only to be perfected by degrees : for it is the organic construction of an internal order of mind, a mental organization, in conformity with the external order of nature, by mutual interaction. It is because it is objective and subjective that it requires the conjoint action of the within and without, that it is a slow progress of organic development, nothing less than the patient construction of a mental fabric formed by minute degrees and slowly accumulating increments through ages of time by the gradual increase of the corpuscular groups in the brain cells.

This is one of the causes of errors of thought and erroneous beliefs, which are now exploded notions because we have instruments of science, and these were long inaccessible to human sense. It therefore may be stated as, or the cause of, the want of means of observation. Another cause is the want of opportunities of observation.

It is obvious that he who has not the opportunity is as ill placed for arriving at a sound conclusion as he who has not the means of observing; to want the opportunity is to want the means. Perhaps at the present time the chief cause of errors is the want of habit or capacity of observation. Although one person may have a better natural aptitude to observe than another, yet no one can observe well in any province of nature without training by practice, any more than he can shoot well without practical lessons.

Thus we get erroneous reasoning by those who exult in the modern diffusion of knowledge, who bray of the enlightenment of the age, and who do not reflect how very small is the minority of men on whom the boasted progress depends actually; how entirely the intellectual possessions of the race have been and are gained and maintained by the few; how little real knowledge the vast majority has, and how mechanical that little is; how great a dead weight of ignorance passively, and how strong an organization of hostile superstition actively, withstand progress. How often has an ingenious pioneer of thought put forth new facts and theories which have met with no acceptance in his day, but which are revived and accepted generations after, because only then has such a raising of the general level of knowledge and such development taken place as render full apprehension and exact expression of his theory possible. People cannot credit the discoverer with having known what he meant, *because it has taken them a hundred years to discover his meaning.*

It cannot be denied that, with respect to the origin and nature of visions and hallucinations, experience makes it plain that phenomena really morbid have uniformly been mistaken for superhuman appearances all the world over. So much lies beyond dispute. Furthermore, it is indisputable that temperaments proved naturally to lapse into morbid action have been designedly selected, and means suited to induce morbid action of them systematically used, in order to obtain visions. But to leap forthwith from that conclusion to the unqualified assertion that all visions of the superhuman everywhere have had a like physiological or pathological origin, and no higher origin, is to make a generalization which will not readily obtain acceptance with our present knowledge of the Periodic Laws of the Corpuscles. It must be instantly and earnestly protested that there are essential differences between the hallucinations of mental disorders and the true superhuman visions of inspired or gifted seership. The vital question really is, whether any vision bears a superhuman superscription on its face, and, if so, what the superscription is. There is one important fact that has to be considered in this argument; that is, we have a physically objective and subjective and demonstrable form of life, living and continuing to live in millions, in the world everywhere, without showing *visibly* to the ordinary power of our eyes. If a hundred years ago anyone had advanced the theory that this life existed and was in many cases the cause of our ailments, describing the whole conditions, he would undoubtedly have been stamped as one suffering from hallucinations and mental disorder. Nevertheless, by the aid of the microscope and aniline dyes we have been able to demonstrate and prove that there is a life of active organisms existing which no one can see without the aid of the "seership" of the microscope, after these organisms have been treated with aniline dyes—not even the microscope alone, however powerful, will enable us to demonstrate as a fact that these exist. Therefore, it is not of any great point in imagination that the common herd of humanity, with their gross material instincts and thoughts, are unable to see the corpuscles of the living spirit that has emaned from the dead human body.

We have truth in Nature as it came from the Divine Creator, and it has to be read with the same unbiased mind, the same open eye, when we inquire as to the universal human good and the Divine interpretation of things; but to find and gain the knowledge of the Truth we must obliterate and cast away the adulterations, the artificial accumulations of centuries of uncontrolled speculation: they mark the impossible of progress. How can it be otherwise with dogmas which depend for their existence on a particular exegesis, with propositions which rest for their evidence upon supposed probabilities, or upon the weight of some unscientific authority which can give no actual proof; with doctrines which every age and nation may make or unmake, which each sect may tamper with, and which anyone may modify for himself?—all of which is totally opposed to the immutable Periodic Laws of the Universe. There is a sense of greatness and solidness about the Periodic Laws of Nature (proved by scientific experiments) which belongs to nothing else. Here at least, amid all the shifting sand of speculation, is one thing sure: unbiased, unprejudiced, uninfluenced by like or dislike, by doubt or fear, the one thing that holds on its way eternally incorruptible and undefiled from eternity;

and this Periodic Law of the Corpuscles proves that the principle of continuity is maintained the same in the Laws of the Spiritual World.

And as regards the proof of Evolution I must say a few words here. Mr. Kidd, in his *The Science of Power* ("The Limits of Darwinism and Social Evolution"), has tried to prove that Darwin was not true in his scientific deductions—or at least only partially so.

I will comment on a few "extracts" from Mr. Kidd's works which will, I contend, prove that Darwin was quite correct and that Mr. Kidd's ideas are erroneous—to say the least; other parts of this work will also prove the errors of Mr. 'Kidd's theory and give the true causes of human evolution.

He asks: "If individual character and racial types are so rigidly fixed by biological inheritance, or inborn heredity, how comes it that the Japanese managed to change their entire national psychology in a single generation?"

They have not changed as types of Homo. They are anatomically and physiologically Stellar Cult people, the same as the Chinese, but have had, in many cases, a mixture introduced of "other blood." But a great number still remain true Stellar Cult type as from the first, before the exodus of these left Old Egypt, their original home. Environment and mixing with other superior races has enabled them to assimilate knowledge which they did not originally possess.

One has only to examine their osteo-anatomy and hair to prove that this is correct. When external objects in many different forms were presented to them continually, the development of the grey matter of their brain would increase from generation to generation, and would be quite sufficient to account for the assimilation of new changes and ideas of what Mr. Kidd calls " national psychology." This, however, has not occurred in one single generation. Their osteo-anatomy has not changed except when there has been a mixture of types, as we find amongst many.[1] The fact that they have assimilated new ideas from an outside race, or races, who are in a higher state of evolution does not prove that Darwin is wrong; on the contrary, we find that the principal change was first produced amongst those who had " mixed " blood, and that the evolution of the corpuscles of the brain cells continues progressively, a point which Mr. Kidd obviously has not taken into any consideration at all; hence his errors. Mr. Kidd recalls the main thesis of his *Social Evolution.* " Civilization rested, it was maintained, not on the intellect, or on the reasoning processes of mind, but on the physical inheritance transmitted from generation to generation, and entirely independent of inborn heredity in the individual," and he states: " None of the leading races or nationalities which have ruled in the past, or which wield power on

[1] See *Origin and Evolution of the Human Race.*

a large scale over other peoples in the present, have done so, or do so now, because of any distinctive superior intellectual faculties inborn in the ruling race."

To sum up:

"Darwinism is the science of the causes which have made those who are efficient in the struggle for their own interests supreme and omnipotent in the world. Now, this doctrine has nothing to do with the science of civilization. It is the doctrine of the efficiency of the animal. It has absolutely nothing to do with the causes making for collective efficiency on the social and moral world founded on mind, which is everything in civilization. Darwinism represents, indeed, the very antithesis of the principles of that social integration which is taking place in civilization. The dividing line, moreover, is fundamental. For the first principle of evolution in the world of the efficient animal of Darwinism is the supremacy and omnipotence therein of individuals, or groups of individuals, efficient in their own interests. The first principle, on the contrary, in the evolution of the social world of civilization lies in the subordination of individuals. The story of creation up to and including human savagery is simply the story of the supremacy in the world of physical force in the life of the individual or the efficient group or the efficient State. But the story of evolution above savagery is nothing else than the story of the gradual rise to supremacy in the world of those psychic forces organized in civilization which are subduing individuals or aggregations efficient in their own interests to those universal principles which are making for the *limitless efficiency of civilization.*"

These statements are absolutely diametrical to facts, and if Mr. Kidd had any real knowledge of the past and present evolution of mankind, I do not think for one moment he would have propounded such theories. Take it as he states:

"The story of creation up to and including human savagery is simply the story of the supremacy in the world of *physical force* in the life of the individual or the efficient group." It is not. The lowest type of human which was evolved from the Anthropoid Ape was the Pygmy; some of these have attained a higher standard than others. The next higher type in evolution is the Masaba Negro; the next higher to that is the non-Hero-Cult Nilotic Negro; the next higher is the Nilotic Negro, with Hero Cult, and from these the Stellar Cult people were evolved. Remnants of all still exist in the world, but what has occurred? This, that the higher type in evolution has exterminated, or driven away into fastnesses, forests, or mountains, the lower types, each in succession. Does he mean to tell me for one moment that "simply *physical force*" was enough to drive the non-Hero Cult away from the Hero Cult? The next higher type were the Stellar Cult people: does he mean to tell me that "physical force" alone was sufficient for these to exterminate the Nilotic Negro? The suggestion is too preposterous to be entertained for one moment. He can prove this, if he cares to make the experiment, by taking a group of Warramunga, or Masai Nilotic Hero Cult people, and a group of Chinese or Japanese, Stellar Cult people: let them fight it out with nothing on—*physical force* would prove his theory was not sound, but that Darwin's was absolutely correct. Why? Because the development of these lower-class humans is as distinct and certain in the evolution of the human race as is the white from the yellow, and the progressive forms of white or dominant races. He states that "Darwinism is the science of the causes which have made those who are efficient in the struggle for their own interests supreme and omnipotent in the world," and then states that the doctrine has nothing to do with civilization, etc. Here again Mr. Kidd fails to recognize what has occurred in the evolution of the human and is entirely wrong in his statement as a result. Man first had short legs, long arms and large abdomen, with small brain—850 to 1,000 c.c. (the Pygmies); next we find great development of bone takes place, longer legs, shorter arms, less abdomen and greater brain—1,000 to 1,200 c.c. (Nilotic Negroes); the next we find is that the bones are not too large, legs, arms and body more proportioned, *and the brain much enlarged*—1,200 to 1,400 c.c. (Stellar Cult people). Had this nothing to do with civilization? The very fact that, as they had greater development of brain tissue, they would observe and think more of all the phenomena of nature, their wants would increase in proportion, and civilization would gradually dawn and take place—this is what has occurred; yet he acknowledges that "collective efficiency in the social and moral world is founded on mind—which is everything in civilization." Quite so; that is the proof of the evolution of the human race. The mind, as he terms it—or, as I would rather state it, the brain cells, and more particularly the grey matter of the brain—had been increasing both in size and thickness as a result of the progressive evolution of the human race, under the Periodic Laws, from the first, and still continues to do so in the higher types of the human. The "series of corpuscles" increase in numbers and complexity; that is progressive evolution according to Darwin's science and is a profound fact. It is owing to the increase of the numbers and complexity of these corpuscles of the brain cells that higher types of evolution in the human race are produced and the highest civilization that has been attained up to the present time has been caused (see later).

Homo first developed great bone and muscular power because he had to contend against large and fierce animals if he was to live and become dominant, which was the Will of the Divine Creator; but as soon as he had overcome these, what did he require for a higher state of evolution? Not more bone and muscles, but brain, and this then began to develop: this is well observed in tracing the Pituitary Gland in the brain from the Pygmy to the Stellar Cult man. With the development of his brain greater powers of thought and observation would come into being. Darwin never left out the development of the brain as a factor to attain a higher state of evolution, and Mr. Kidd's works, therefore, are most decidedly misleading as regards the truth of evolution anatomically or socially: he must have overlooked what Darwin's opinion was when the latter wrote as follows: "Variability is generally related to the condition of life to which each species has been exposed during several successive generations; changed conditions act in two ways, directly on the whole organization or *on certain parts alone*, and indirectly through the reproductive system." As the wants of man increased so did his power of reasoning.

The progressive development of the grey matter of the brain produced, as a result, "ideas and reasoning powers" to a far greater extent than man had attained before, giving him knowledge which he formerly did not possess. As one example, it would enable him to form and acquire new implements, which the inferior races were unable to fashion, thus enabling him to dominate and exterminate any resistance on the part of his inferiors. Science and Art would gradually dawn, and a higher and nobler form of religious ethics and civilization would be the result. Civilization, it is true, is an arbitrary term. Anthropologists have not yet settled the boundary line between a savage and a civilized people. The obtaining food from wild plants and animals, without any of the arts of culture and domestication, would apply as a definition to the savagism of the aborigines of Australia and all the non-Hero Cult people and probably to most of the Hero Cult people as well. But when we come to the group of the Masai, we must admit that an early step in civilization had commenced which has continued progressively ever since. But what does Darwin say in his *The Descent of Man*?—"The small strength and speed of man, his want of natural weapons, etc., are more than counter-balanced, firstly, by his *intellectual powers*, through which he has formed for himself weapons, tools, etc.; secondly, by his social qualities, which lead him to give and receive aid from his fellow-men. Natural selection had been the chief agent of change, though largely aided by the inherited effects of habit and also slightly by the direct action of the fluids of the system having altered for some special purpose (products of ductless glands), inducing other changes. In regard *to mental powers the faculties have been chiefly, or even exclusively, gained for the benefit of the community, and the individuals,*" therefore, have at the same time gained an advantage indirectly. The social instincts, together with sympathy (which leads to our regarding the approbation and disapprobation of others), have served as the primary impulse and guides. As the wants of man increased, so did his power of reasoning. Social instincts have been acquired by natural selection, or the indirect result of other instincts and faculties, such as sympathy, reason, experience, and a tendency to imitation, or long-continued habit. Man is a social being, but social instincts never existed in all of the same species; he would inherit a tendency to be faithful to his comrades and obedient to the leader of his tribe, but these are qualities common to most social animals; and although man has no special instincts to tell him how to aid his fellow-men, he still has the impulse, and with his improved intellectual faculties naturally would be much guided in this respect by reason and experience. With highly civilized nations, continued progress depends, in a subordinate degree, on natural selection; for such nations do not supplant and exterminate one another as do savage tribes. Nevertheless, the more intelligent members within the same community will succeed better in the long run than the inferior, and leave a more numerous progeny; and this is a form of natural selection. The more efficient causes of progress seem to consist of a good education during youth, *whilst the brain is impressible*, and a high standard of excellence, inculcated by the ablest and best men, embodied in the laws, customs and traditions of the nation and enforced by public opinion. With man we can see no definite limit to the continued development of the brain and mental faculties. It should be borne in mind that the enforcement of public opinion depends on our appreciation of the approbation and disapprobation of others: and this appreciation is founded on our sympathy, which hardly can be doubted originally was developed through natural selection as one of the most important elements of the social instincts.

I think what I have written here and in my other work is sufficient to prove that Mr. Kidd's theories are not the truth of the matter and that Darwin was perfectly right in his deductions. For further proofs, for those interested in Darwin's theory, I would refer them to *The Descent of Man*, new edition, 1901.

Many readers may not agree with my chronology, and may think that I am not correct in dating back the world's history and the age of man to such great antiquity. But let me assure them recent discoveries prove my assertions. One example alone is sufficient for this, viz. the discovery of skeletons of the Stellar Cult type of man found in the Pliocene strata in Lombardy. It is important to remember that the skeletons found in this stratum were of the modern type of man; proofs that they were Stellar Cult people were found buried with them, as well as their osteo-anatomy: that they lived and died at this period, and were not accidental burials, we have Professor Sergi's authority—a most unimpeachable one. The Pliocene strata were formed at least 600,000 years ago.

The obstruction to the acceptance of the inductive evidence on which alone a lasting knowledge of ethnology and of the antiquity of the human race can be had is the same which opposed the progress of the science of Geology, and retarded for centuries the demonstration of the causes which in the long course of ages modified the crust of the earth—"incompatibility," namely, "with the chronology of the Bible." It must be admitted by everyone that there is much uncertainty as to Sacred Chronology being correct, to say the least about it.

The thirst for power is never satisfied. It is always insatiable, both in men and nations. When Rome was the mistress of the world, the Emperors caused themselves to be worshipped as gods. The Church of Rome claimed despotism over the soul, and over the whole life from the cradle to the grave. It gave and sold absolutions for past and future sins. It claimed to be infallible in matters of faith. It decimated America to convert the Mexicans and Peruvians, and what is the Church of Rome now? Still carrying on the same old game, or trying to, amongst a more enlightened people. In rare instances the knowledge of immortality through a definite personal experience has been obtained before death, and it has been the priceless jewel obtained by the living of a life in accord with the highest ideals of nature, justice and morality of the individual, but never by those ignorant and despotic men, those carping critics, who have aggregated themselves into large organizations and would by iron rule and despotic power subject to their domination and control all other humans and destroy all individuality.

Many men have it in their power, if they really try, to find out true religion and separate it from the false; so also have they then, when they have attained this, the power to enter "the Mysteries of the Ancient Egyptians" and to converse with the spirits of the ancestors; but the majority will not try, and they remain forever ignorant and forever outside. Therefore, how much reliance can be placed upon those ignorant men who deny altogether that which they have never tried to attain?—yet that is what the present human does. A man who clings to sensuals cannot associate with spirituals. A man who relies only on his common sense, on his money-getting power, or on his mere energy after good dinners, will never reach the higher and spiritual planes, which, however, are not less real because they are unseen of such. If we want the truth, we must labour for it quite as hard as we labour for gold.

Most people cannot believe that the self-identity of the individual intelligence (the spirit) can be demonstrated this side of the grave; but, as St. Paul states, "There is a natural body and there is a spiritual body," and that is true, and can be demonstrated by those who have learnt the mysteries.

Knowledge of man's being is the highest of all possessions, the highest of all knowledge, and the knowledge the world needs most to-day. It is the knowledge with which men can do the most good in all the activities of life.

> These things shall be. A loftier race
> Than e'er the world hath known shall rise,
> With flame of freedom in their souls
> And light of knowledge in their eyes.—ANON.

CHAPTER III

SIGN LANGUAGE

SIGN LANGUAGE, the earliest of all languages which Homo used, consisted of Gesture Signs, which were accompanied with a few appropriate sounds, which may be termed words; but even before man existed we can trace certain sounds or words back to man's predecessors. The Cynocephalus, for example, has eight or nine different sounds or words.

In this Sign Language they acted their wants and wishes in expressive pantomime whilst wearing the skins of animals—" Myth-making Man " did not create the gods in his own image.

The primary divinities of Egypt, such as Set, Horus and Shu, three of the earliest, were represented in the likeness of the Hippopotamus, the Crocodile and the Lion, Ptah as a Beetle, Taht as an Ibis, and Seb as a Goose. They are likenesses of powers that were superhuman, not human. So it was with the goddesses. Apt was imaged as a Water-cow, Heket as a Frog, Rannut as a Serpent, Hathor as a Fruit-tree.

Totemism was formulated by myth-making man with types that were the very opposite of human, and in mythology the anthropomorphic representation was preceded by the whole menagerie of Totemic Zootypes.

If primitive man had projected the shadow of himself upon external nature, to shape its elemental forces in his own image, or if the unfeatured Vast had unveiled to him any likeness of the human face, then the primary representation of the Nature Powers (which became the later divinities) ought to have been anthropomorphic, and the likeness reflected in the mirror of the most ancient mythologies should have been human, whereas the Powers and Divinities were first represented by animals, birds and reptiles. The Sun and Moon were not considered "human in their nature" when one was imaged as a Crocodile, a Lion, a Bull, a Beetle or a Hawk, and the other as a Hare, a Frog, an Ape or an Ibis, as they are represented in the Egyptian hieroglyphics by means of the Zootypes. Until Har-Ur, the Elder Horus, had been depicted as the Child in place of the Calf or Lamb, the Fish, of shoot of the Papyrus plant (which was comparatively late), there was no human figure personalized in the mythology of Egypt. Mythology did not spring from fifty or a hundred sources, as frequently assumed. It is one as a system of representation,.one as a mould of thought, one as a mode of expression, and all its great primordial types are virtually universal. Neither do the myths that were inherited and which were repeated for ages by the later races of men afford any direct criterion of the intellectual status of such races. Mythology has had an almost limitless descent. It was in a savage or primitive state in the most ancient Egypt, but the Egyptians who continued to repeat the myths in Sign Language did not remain savages. Egyptian mythology is the oldest in the world, and it did not begin as an explanation of natural phenomena, but as a representation by such means as were available at the time. No better definition of "myth" or "mythology" could be given than is conveyed by the Egyptian word "Sem." This signifies "representation on the ground of likeness," which led to all the forms of Sign Language that ever could be employed.

In the folk-lore of various races the human soul takes the form of a snake, a mouse, a hawk, a pigeon, a bee, a jackal, or other animal, each of which was an Egyptian Zootype of some power or soul in Nature before there was any representation of the human soul or ancestral spirit in the human form. Hence we are told that when twins were born, the Batavians believed that one of the pair was a crocodile.

Mr. Spencer accepts this "belief" and asks: "May we not conclude that twins, of whom one gained the name of Crocodile, gave rise to a legend which originated this monstrous belief?" (*Data of Sociology*, chap. 22, par. 175). But all such representations are mythical, and are not to be explicated by the theory of "monstrous belief." It is a matter of Sign Language. The Batavians knew as well as we that no crocodile was ever born twin together with a human child. In this instance they were asserting in their primitive way that man is born with or as a soul. This the gnosis enables us to prove. One of the earliest types of the Sun as a Soul of Life in the water is a crocodile. We see the Mother who brings forth a crocodile when the Goddess Neith is portrayed in human shape as the suckler of the young crocodiles hanging to her breasts. Neith is a wet-nurse personified whose child was the young Sun-god. As Sebek he was imaged by the Crocodile that emerged from the waters at sunrise. Sebek was at once the child and the Crocodile brought forth by the Great Mother in the mythology. And because the crocodile had imaged a soul of life in water as a superhuman power, it became a representation in Sign Language of the human soul. We see this same type of a soul in external nature applied to the human soul in the *Ritual of Resurrection* of Ancient Egypt, when the Osiris in the Nether World exclaims, "I am the crocodile in the form of a man," that is, as a soul of which the crocodile had been a symbol, as Soul of the Sun. It was thus the crocodile was born with the child as a matter of Sign Language, not as a belief.

Mr. Spencer not only argues for the actuality of these "beliefs" concerning natural facts supposed to have been held by primitive men and scientific Egyptians, which vanish with a true interpretation of the mythical mode of representation; he further insists that there seems to be "ample justification for the belief that any kind of creature may be transformed into any other," because of the metamorphosis observed in the insect world, or elsewhere, from which there resulted "the theory of metamorphosis in general" and the notion "that things of all kinds may suddenly change their forms," man included, of course (*Data*, chap. 8, par. 557). But there was no evidence throughout all nature to suggest that any kind of creature could be transformed into any other kind. On the contrary, nature showed them that the frog was a *tadpole continued*; that the chrysalis was the prior status of the butterfly, and that the Old Moon changed into the New. The transformation was visible and invariable, and the period of transformation was always the same in kind. There was no sign or suggestion of an unlimited possibility in metamorphosis. Neither was there ever a race of savages who did think or believe (in the words of Mr. Spencer) "that any kind of creature may be transformed into any other," no more than there ever were boys who believed that any kind of bird could lay any other kind of bird's egg. They are too good observers for any such self-delusion as that.

Innumerable examples might be here set forth showing how Sign Language was first used by primitive man to express his ideas in Zootype form, and then carried on by the Stellar Cult people in their astro-mythology to represent the Elemental Powers, and even still later into the Solar, before he had formed language enough to express adequately his " mental pictures," in terminology of the present day. I trust that which I have written (*supra*) is sufficient to enable my Brothers to follow and understand the evolution that has taken place in the development of nature's education of Homo. If further information on the subject is desired by any Brother, I would refer him to my friend the late Gerald Massey's great work *Ancient Egypt, The Light of the World.* No one since the old Urshi of Egypt has so thoroughly expounded the truths on this subject as he, and I have quoted freely from his great work.

CHAPTER IV

CREATION AND EVOLUTION TO PYGMIES—PRE-TOTEMIC HOMO, WITH ORIGIN OF THE FIRST SYMBOL

" In the beginning, God created." We find various tales of creation in many lands past and present, but the so-called legends of creation would be more correctly termed the Legend of Human Evolution. In speaking of the creation of the human race I shall confine myself to two kinds—the same as you find in the V.S.L. The first was the creation of Life caused by certain combinations of Series of Corpuscles—the number and the series are known to T.G.A.O.T.U. only—and a progressive evolution of these from the beginning by an increase both of numbers and series, until we find the first Homo evolved from an anthropoid ape in Africa. And it was in Africa that man was first born, as I shall prove. Progressive evolution to a higher type and state still continues, and whatever man does—or may do—he can never stop this. By ignoring and disobeying the Laws of T.G.A.O.T.U. he may retard it in some families or branches of the human race. The consequence, however, is the destruction of that nation and a set-back, to begin again, wherever this occurs. But other nations—other branches of the human race—will take on the progressive action, and, if the laws made by man are good, will assist this.

The whole of this progressive evolution, as well as devolution, is governed by the Periodic Laws of the Corpuscles, which are God's little bricks, with which He builds the Universe and all that therein is.

We will, therefore, for our argument, begin with the first human evolved—how many millions of years ago it is impossible to state, but his implements have been found below the Miocene strata (Oligocene), therefore several, at least. His implements being there, he must have been in existence at the time of the formation of the strata.

This first man was the little Pygmy. His descendants are still found in many different parts of the world—in South America, China, Malay, New Guinea and probably other places—but the majority are still living in Africa, where his original home was, and is, around and near the Great Lakes at the head of the Nile.

The Pygmy is the lowest type of the human and has the smallest brain of any man—850 c.c. The Pygmies have no records or traditions of the past, no fetish or Totemic rites. They have no Totems, no signs of tattoo scored on their bodies,

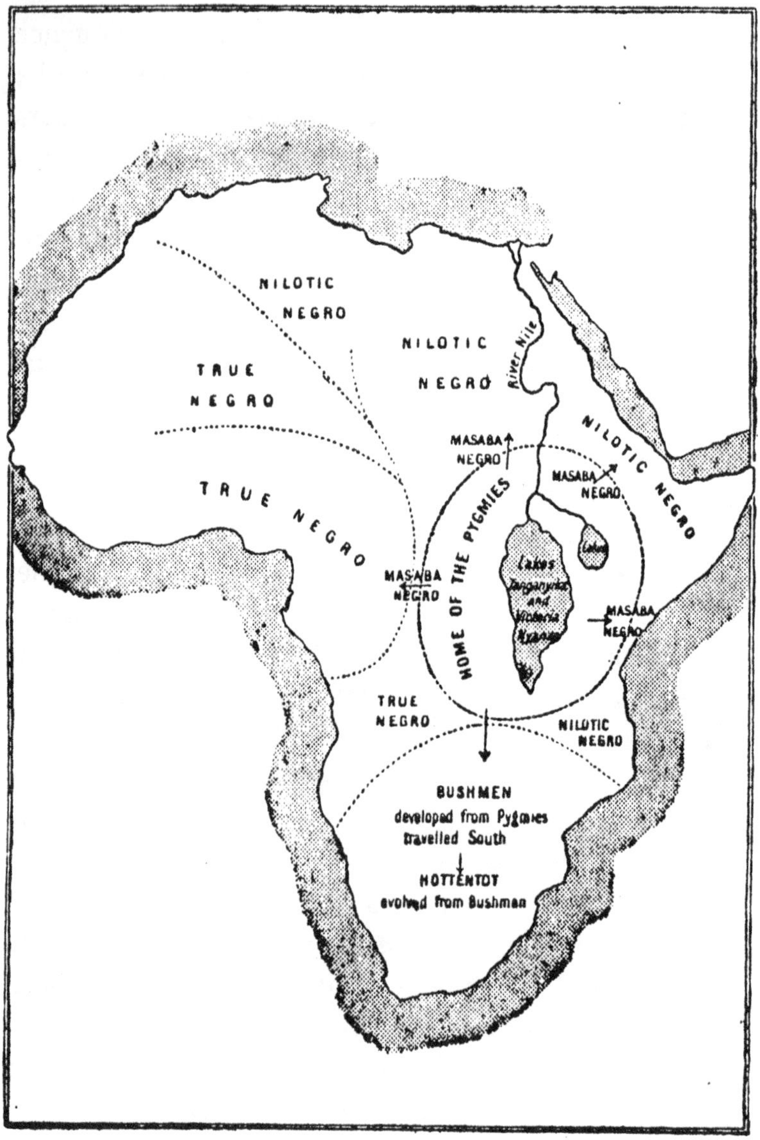

Map of Africa.

Showing the home of Primary Man.

no rites of puberty, no eating of the parent in honour of a primitive sacrament. They have longer arms by 1 per cent. than the white man.

The hair, lips, abdomen of the Pygmy are all characteristic.

He has a language of his own—but a few words, about 100.

I believe that I am the first man to prove this to be true.

He speaks or communicates principally by signs and symbols, i.e. a Gesture and Sign Language.

The earliest human language consisted of gesture signs, which were accompanied with a few appropriate sounds, some of which were traceably continued from the predecessors of man.

In this Sign Language, which was earlier than words, they acted their wants and wishes in expressive pantomime whilst wearing the skins of animals that were pursued for food. Dancing, for example, was a mode of Sign Language in all the Mysteries. To know certain Mysteries implied the ability to dance them when they could not be otherwise explained.

The Egyptian wisdom registered the fact that the Pygmy was the earliest human, because the earliest divine man known in their mythology is portrayed as a Pygmy.

Following the Zootypes, the primitive form of the Elder Horus was that of Bes. Bes is a figure of the Child Horus in the likeness of a Pygmy, and Bes-Horus is the earliest form of the Pygmy Ptah. Also the seven powers which co-operate with Ptah are represented as seven Pygmies.

Moreover, Ptah, the divine primitive man, is the imperfect progenitor of the perfect man in his son Atum or Adam.

From Africa the Pygmy spread all over the world; we know this because we find his implements there, and some descendants in a few places.

He has a belief in a Supreme Being, and an after or spirit life. He propitiates the Supreme Being, the spirits of his ancestors, and also the Elementary Powers.

One of the implements we use in the Lodge originated with these Pygmies—the first that comes into operation when we open the Lodge, the *gavel*. This was an original sacred sign and symbol—and still is—of the Pygmies, and represents with them, the same as with us, the Great One, the Chief, the Master. The Pygmy symbol in its original form is this , just three sticks crossed. But how many hundreds of years passed before the original Pygmies were able to form this I do not know. Following the evolution of this symbol we can trace its development into two or three forms, which I will depict as we proceed to the higher types of man.

The gavel, therefore, may be considered the

first and oldest sign, symbol or implement that we use, and its origin was the sacred Pygmy symbol. The Pygmies that travelled South from their original home developed into the Bushman, and these latter into the Hottentot. These inhabit South Africa: they never came North, and never left Africa; none of their remains have ever been found outside the southern part of Africa.

Those Pygmies that went West, North and East developed into the Masaba Negro; none of these Masaba Negroes have ever been found outside Africa, but some of the original descendants are still there.

All these are pre-Totemic and non-anthropophagous. The Masaba Negro in the West developed into the true Negro. These never left Africa as an exodus—only carried away as slaves. They are still there, and are the true Negroes. No higher development has ever taken place in this branch of the human.

The Masaba Negroes in the North and East developed into the Nilotic Negro, and this was the branch of the human race that evolved into higher types in evolution. The Bushman, Hottentot and Masaba Negroes are the connecting links from the Pygmy and are found in Africa only. This is a positive proof that Man was evolved in Africa and not Asia or any other part of the world.[1]

No signs or symbols that we use were evolved

[1] See *Origin and Evolution of Primitive Man.*

or originated from these connecting links or from the true Negro.

There is a great difference anatomically between the Nilotic Negro and the true Negro.

With the Nilotic Negro came into existence what may be termed "the Second Creation"—the cutting and opening, the making of men and women. Hitherto all had been a promiscuous herd; now, at the inception of their Totemic ceremonies, the boy was made into a man and the girl into a woman. This is the origin and meaning of the second creation in the V.S.L.

Thus the creation of man was mystical in one sense and in another Totemic, i.e. pre-Totemic and Totemic—pre-human and human. By Totemism we mean the earliest formation of society, in which the human group was first discreted from the gregarious horde that grovelled together previously in animal promiscuity.

It is in Totemism only that we can trace the natural genesis of various doctrines and dogmas that have survived to be looked upon as a Divine Revelation especially vouchsafed to later times, in consequence of their having been continued as religious Mysteries without the guidance of the primitive gnosis.

Totemism originated in Sign Language rather than sociology, the signs being afterwards applied for use in sociology, as they were in mythology and fetishism.

Ceremonial rites were established as the means of memorizing facts in Sign Language when there were no written records of the human past. In these the knowledge was acted: the ritual was exhibited and kept in ever-living memory by continual repetition. The Mysteries, Totemic or religious, were founded on the basis of action.

Thus the sign to the eye and the sound to the ear were continued *pari passu* in the dual development of Sign Language, that was both visual and vocal at the same time when the brothers and sisters were identifying themselves, *not with, or as, animals, but by means of them, and by making use of them as Zootypes for their Totems*

CHAPTER V

EVOLUTION OF TOTEMIC PEOPLE AND ORIGIN OF SOME OF OUR SIGNS, SYMBOLS, CEREMONIES, AND EXPLANATIONS OF THE SAME

THE first evolution from the Masaba Negro along the Great African Lakes and the banks of the Nile was the non-Hero Cult people, and from these developed a higher type—the Hero Cult Nilotic Negroes.

The non-Hero Cult people followed the Pygmies in their migration all over the world, killed them wherever they came into opposition, and drove the others into the mountains, forests and not very accessible parts, where we find them isolated at the present day—because they did not follow them there.

Later the Hero Cult Nilotic Negroes followed the non-Hero Cult people and migrated in their tracks, but did not war against them or kill them, except they had committed some act against the Law of Tabu, but drove them away from the best and most fertile lands and hunting grounds and occupied these themselves.

The osteo-remains and implements of these are found in most parts of the world where they migrated—and the two classes can easily be distinguished from each other by their osteo-anatomy. Some of their descendants are still living in Africa and other countries. Both the non-Hero Cult and the Hero Cult—as example, Australia, New Guinea, New Zealand, North and South America, many parts of Asia and the Pacific Islands—all practise Totemic rites and are Androphagi, or were at first ; a few are still.

These are the Totemic people in different states of evolution, and their governments and laws were, and are, pure Socialism.

Totemic Sociology, therefore, was the first kind of government established by primitive man.

They believe in a Great Spirit, spirits of their ancestors and Elemental Powers, all of which they propitiate.

The curious and important fact I wish my readers to note particularly is, that neither these nor the Stellar Cult people, who were the next to follow them from Africa, ever developed into a higher type of Homo by evolution outside Africa. Only those who remained in Old Egypt of the Hero Cult people developed by evolution into the Stellar Cult people, and these by progressive evolution into the Lunar and then Solar. All before the Hero Cult were hunters only, but these in Africa began to tame wild animals and commenced agriculture, they formed the primary towns by building huts of mud, reeds and wood, built ramparts and dug fosses around to protect themselves from wild animals. Their brains were increased to 1,250 c.c., and they developed their language to 800 or 900 words. The two types of Nilotic Negroes are easily distinguished by the evolution that took place in their osteo-anatomy, as well as by many physiological points too numerous to enter into in detail in this book.

Some of the signs and symbols we use originated amongst these Nilotic Negroes. *But please do not fall into the error of thinking that these people ever knew anything about Freemasonry. They did not, but they instituted their Totemic ceremonies and used signs and symbols in their sacred ceremonies to represent in Sign Language what they could not say in words, because at that early time they had not developed terminology to express all their ideas and the superhuman powers of Nature which they had observed. The signs and symbols have been handed down from generation to generation, and that is why we have used them.* We can now express in words what were "mental pictures" to them.

The penal sign in the First Degree is one—and is still used by these Nilotic Negroes at the present day. In all courts of justice in some parts of Africa they make use of this sign instead of the V.S.L. They have never been known to break their oath after using this sign. The sign used by Brothers of the R.A. on entering their Lodge was, and is, the same sign that is still used and given before any member can enter their camp when certain Totemic ceremonies are performed. Another sign used in the 18° H.D.H.A. is one that is always used by the Hero Cult people all over the world—North and South America, New Guinea and Pacific Isles, as well as in Africa. The two Pillars, or two Poles, which they use in their ceremonies , representing with them the North and South Pole Stars and the North and South divisions of heaven, were the origin of the S. and J.W. columns, and were the originals of the two pillars at the porchway entrance to all the temples in the world in the Stellar, Lunar and Solar Cults, including K.S., as I shall prove.

These two pillars or poles still survive amongst some of the descendants of the Nilotic Negroes in many parts of the world—as, for example, amongst the Arunta of Central Australia.[1] These people have no North Pole Star, or North division of heaven, but they still continue to carry the two symbolic poles about with them, which they erect

[1] See Spencer and Gillen, *The Native Tribes of Central Australia* and *The Northern Tribes of Central Australia.*

wherever they go, as a *sign of locality or encampment,* both of which are limited to the North and South. One is called Nurtunga ; this is the North Pole of the two and is never met with in the South. The other is called Warringa and is always located in the South. The Nurtunga is typical of the Northern and the Warringa of the Southern part of the Arunta tribes.

Each of them, like the Egyptian Tatt pillars, is a *sign of establishing or founding*—as is shown from its use in the ceremony of "young men making."

The Nilotic Negroes knew that this  was the sacred sign for "The Great One" amongst the Pygmies, and they converted it into two different forms. First they placed the two sticks across  thus forming a double cross, and later added another, thus 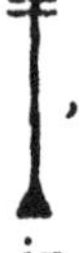, forming the treble cross. These are still used in the same two forms by Brothers of the 33°. I give you the origins and can trace them for you through all the Cults up to the present day.

It was a very sacred sign amongst the Hero Cult people and is one of the symbols for their chief hero.

A second phase of the Pygmy sign was its conversion into the Sacred Axe 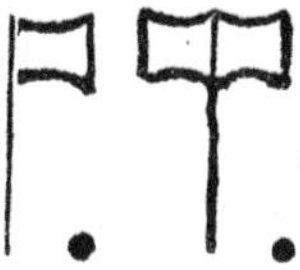, when stones took the place of sticks—as being more effective in use—by the hafting in the first place of a stone into a wooden handle and later forming an axe of metal.

It represents amongst them "The Great Chief," sometimes called "The Great Chief of the Hammer," and the Sacred Axe was another symbol for Horus, their chief hero, and later for "Horus of the Double Horizon" or "Cleaver of the Way" in the first Solar Cult.

Another ceremony, part of the initiation, called the Bora, is practised by the Hero Cult Nilotic Negroes, and is the original of our 3°, which ceremony has been much perverted from the true, but is more faithfully portrayed in part of the 18°; all the members are pledged to secrecy. The penalty for any breach of its rules is death. "A valley of death" is portrayed, and members in two rows, armed with spears and clubs, etc., form an arch over a representative dead body. (Photograph of the same in second edition of *Signs and Symbols of Primordial Man*, p. 455.) The initiate is conducted through this "valley of death" and has to undergo trials, etc. His conductor carries implements of power and might to ward off all dangers. As he arrives at each

Brother, they say, "I will not let thee pass until you give me the word," with threats of death. The word is given as he passes each, and he is conducted through safely.

It is a primitive symbolic and dramatic form of passing through the underworld. He is initiated into the passage of the dead to the spirit world—a Totemic form of the "Abyss" of the Stellar and Lunar Cult people and Amenta of the Solar in the Eschatology. Another proof that the aboriginal Australians were Hero Cult Nilotic Negroes may be found in some of the words they use—for example (in their "Snake" ceremony), "Ara Tapa Tyiri ai," the meaning of which they have forgotten. This is pure Ancient Egyptian, and means "The chief of the Red Crown made, or constructed, another burial-place for the Snake," and is represented by the Egyptian Tem, who in one form was symbolically depicted as a Snake, as the God of the East—Tem-Asar in the East and Tem-Ra in the West—and in the V.S.L. we see that Moses lifted up the serpent in the wilderness (Num. xxi. 9), showing that he was "wise" in the Stellar Cult doctrines and that the symbolism had been brought on from the Wallunga Totemic ceremony.

These Nilotic Negroes were the first of the human race to smelt iron ore and work in metals. The Kavirondo and Gemi were the tribes, and still are, who performed and discovered this and carry on the art to this day. Their chief hero was called Horus-Behutet, or the Great Blacksmith, one of his names. That—his name—is the original word for the first artificer in metals, and not T.C., which is a Hebrew substituted one. They (the Nilotic Negroes) formed a society which still exists amongst them and is divided into two classes—the Operatives, i.e. the artizans, the workers, and the Priests, who possess a secret cult; each was, and is, separate, but have some signs and symbols in common. The Pygmies, Bushmen, Hottentots and Masaba Negroes are all pre-Totemic and, therefore, non-sociological.

The Nilotic Negroes were, and are, all Totemic, and their form of government is Totemic Sociology —a true Socialism.

All may be classed as Palæolithic, i.e. their instruments were not polished. The Pygmies' were chipped on one side only and they could not haft. The Nilotic Negroes' were chipped on both sides, and they had learnt the art of hafting.

The Hero Cult people travelled along the Valley of the Nile, came North, and gradually evolved into a higher type of man.

The Stellar Cult people were so called because they kept their time by the observation of the recession of the seven Pole Stars or Little Bear, which later they named the "Seven Glorious Ones." These seven have been brought on through the Stellar, Lunar and Solar Cults and into the Christian doctrines under various names and types, and are the originals of all our sevens.

Amongst the *Totemic people* the seven Powers were elemental; these became divinized in the mythology as children or sons of the old Earth Mother under many names, now divinized as Apt, uranographically represented in the constellation of the Great Bear, or Ursa Major, and in the astro-mythology became the Gods of the Pole Star, with Horus in Ursa Minor.

In the Stellar Mythos the seven Powers are symbolically represented by the seven Stars of Ursa Minor, and are called the Seven Glorious Ones with Horus.

In the Lunar Cult the seven Powers are the seven Taasu with Taht.

In the Solar Mythos the seven Powers are the seven Khammu with Ptah.

In the Eschatology the seven Powers that pass through various phases, always in groups of seven, are the seven souls of man, which finally become the seven gifts of the Holy Spirit.

Thus there were seven primary Powers in the mythical and astronomical phases, six of whom are represented by Zootypes and the seventh is imaged in the likeness of a man. This is repeated in the Eschatology, where the highest soul of seven is the Ka-eidolon, with a human face and figure as the final type of spirit, which was human on the earth and is to be eternal in heaven.

The *Ritual* states (chap. 85): "My image is eternal."

According to native traditions the eagle-hawk and crow were first among the ancestors of the human race. It is the same in the Kamite mythology. The two primary elements were those of darkness and light:

Set was the power of darkness; Horus the power of light.

In one representation, the two elements were imaged by means of the black bird of Set and the white bird, or Golden Hawk, of Horus, portrayed back to back. These two birds are equated by the black cockatoo and the white cockatoo as the two Totems of the Mukjarawaint in Western Australia.

Thus we can identify the two primal Elemental Powers which are universal in mythology, and these two Powers, or animistic souls, were divinized as the two gods Set and Horus—that is, as the first two Elemental Powers which became the non-human ancestors in mythology.

They are also known as the creators who divided the Murray Blacks into two classes or brotherhoods, whose Totems were the Eagle-hawk and Crow, and who now shine as stars in the sky.

These two Australian souls or spirits of the two primary Elements can be paralleled in the two souls that are assigned to man, or the Manes, in the tradition of certain aboriginal races, called the dark shade and the light shade, the first two souls of the seven in the *Ritual*. These, as Egyptian, are two of the seven elements from which the enduring soul and total personality of man is finally reconstructed in the Mysteries of Amenta, after death.

They are the dark shade, called the Khabsu, and the light shade, called the Sahu.

In the Mythos, Horus is divinized as the white god. The children of Horus are the Khuti in the Stellar Cult, and in the Eschatology the Khuti are "the Glorious Ones," which must be distinguished from "the Glorified," the latter being the ancestors and once human on earth; the former were non-human or animistic spirits and powers divinized.

With the Blacks of Australia the secret "wisdom" is the same as that of the Nilotic Negroes in Africa.

In the Christian Cult the seven have been brought on from the Eschatology. These seven, as seven periods of the world's existence, have been brought on in the 18°, but the *Ritual* of this part of the 18°, as given, has no meaning, the true gnosis of which was the periods of time of the recession of each star of Ursa Minor; to recommence or begin again after the seventh had fallen down in the waters of space.

It is these elemental souls that have been mixed up with the human souls by Hindus, Greeks, Buddhists, and Pythagoreans after the true gnosis of the Egyptian Mystery Teachers had become lost and perverted, and mistaken for the human soul in course of transmigration through the series, which were but representatives of souls distinguished as non-human by those who understood Sign Language. There is not, and never will be, any transmigration of human souls, and this is also where the translators of the Book of Enoch have erred, "The sons of God who cohabited with the daughters of men." The translator or writer of this book mixes the seven Elemental Powers, which were divinized, or the mythical gods, with the human women, not understanding the Sign Language of the *Ritual* (cp. Gen. vi. 1–4).

These Stellar Cult people learnt the art of polishing and were the earliest of what have been called the Neolithic people.

The terms Stone Age, Iron Age, and Bronze Age, which are still used by present-day scientists, are very misleading as indicating the true evolution of mankind with regard to time and types, because even with the early Hero Cult Nilotic Negro, in Africa at least, man had learnt the method of smelting iron ore and the art of making spears and arrow-heads. I leave it an open question if these people carried on this art outside Africa. I have up to the present time found no evidence that they did, but only "chipped" their implements on both sides.

Bronze was undoubtedly manufactured by the

Stellar Cult people. The proof of iron and bronze having been used by these Stellar Cult people (Neolithic people) may be seen by some of their works cut on hard stones in the various temples and the remains of the implements found in many parts where Stellar people migrated, especially in South America.

That we do not find many iron and bronze implements of the earlier dates is not to be wondered at; it would be more surprising if we did, as obviously these would oxidize and become obliterated within a few thousand years at most, wherever exposed to moist air and water.

No doubt many implements of stone were used up to a very late date; probably they did not find the materials at first in the open country to which they migrated, and so were unable to manufacture any metal instruments, therefore continued to use primitive stone. Obviously the terms Stone Age, Iron Age and Bronze Age cannot have any true meaning with regard to the types and times in the evolution of the human race that these terms are supposed to represent, and are absolutely illogical and misleading in such a sense, and I wish to emphasize this in opposition to all the Professors of the present day.

The only true divisions are:—

Pre-Totemic

Totemic { (1) Non-Hero Cult
(2) Hero Cult }

and

Stellar }
Lunar } Cults
Solar }

as the anatomical and physiological conditions correspond with the various Cults, as well as language, arts and sciences, allowing of course for overlapping that took place in some countries during the evolution from one to the other.

The distinguishing characteristics are absolutely certain and non-misleading, as I have shown in this and other of my works.

Their tradition is that *all descended* from the Mount, i.e. the Mount of the Pole, first represented by the South Pole, when Set, or El Shadai, was the name given to the Primary Deity when they dwelt South of the Equator, and after by the North, when the name of Horus was that of the Primary God and had replaced Set. As these people who travelled North from the region South of the Equator arrived at Apta, or the Equator, where the two Pole Stars were seen to be equally on the horizon, the two then were equal, and were represented symbolically as two Eyes, two Poles, two Jackals, and other dual types. As they still travelled North, the South Pole Star sank down in the waters of space and the North Pole Star rose in the heavens; then the North Pole Star symbolized Horus, who became the Primary Deity. This corresponds to the later Stellar and early Solar

Cult, as we read in the V.S.L., to Ihuh and Ihu, the Egyptian Hu or Neb-Huhi, or Hebrew Ishi: "Thou shalt call me Ishi; and shalt call me no more Baali"=Set (Hos. ii. 16).

This tradition of descending from the Mount is one point of distinction from the Solar people, whose tradition is that they *ascended* from below, or from Amenta.

Here we find the true origin of H.D.H.A. as used by Brothers of the 18°. The Stellar Cult people may justly be said to have founded Old Egypt, and divided it first into seven Nomes, or Domains, with a chief or prince over each. The original Nomes were allotted to seven different Totemic Tribes, representing the Elemental Powers, and were known by their Totems—badges or banners—as distinguishing emblems. As they progressed in evolution, other Nomes were added, making twelve; later more. The twelve Totems or badges of the Nomes are the originals of the banners used by the R.A.M.

The Hero Cult mythology of the Nilotic Negro was now evolved into *astro-mythology* by divinizing the Elemental Powers and giving each a star on high.

The types in Sign Language had been formulated in Totemism, and were first employed to distinguish the Motherhoods and the Brotherhoods, and re-applied to the Elemental Powers in mythology, and afterwards (now in the Stellar Cult) repeated in the constellations as uranographic figures or pictures, as modes of record in the heavens with a view of determining time and seasons and registering the prehistoric past. The stars were used by the Egyptians to illustrate the mysteries that were out of sight.

Their brains had developed and become enlarged to 1,400 to 1,500 c.c.

In Totemism, the Mother and Motherhoods, the Sister and Sisterhoods, the Brother and Brotherhoods, the girl who transformed at puberty, the mother who was eaten as a sacrifice, the two women who were ancestresses, were all of them human, all of them actual, in the domain of natural fact. But when the same characters have been contained in mythology, they are superhuman. The Mother and Motherhoods, the Sister and Sisterhoods, the Brother and Brotherhoods, have been divinized. The realities of Totemism have supplied the types to mythology as goddesses and gods that wear the heads or skins of beasts to denote their character. The mother as human, in Totemism, was known as the Water-cow, and this became the type of the Great Mother in mythology and polytheism. But it was the *type* that was continued, not the *human mother*. The mother as first person in the human family was the first person in the Totemic Sociology. Thence came the Great Mother in mythology, who was fashioned in the Matriarchal mould, but with this difference:

it is the human mother underneath the mask in Totemism. It was *not* the human mother who was divinized as the Great Provider in mythology. Thus, the mother was human in the mask of Totemism and was superhuman in the mask of mythology. The human mother might be represented by, or as, the Totemic cow, serpent, frog or vulture; nevertheless they were not human mothers who were divinized in those same likenesses as the Egyptian Goddesses Isis, Rannut, Hekat and Neith. But the human mother who was eaten alive at the sacramental meal did supply a type of the superhuman mother in external nature, who also gave herself as a voluntary sacrifice for human food and sustenance—the Mother of life in death, who furnished the first eucharist that was eaten in the religious mysteries. The human mother had been an actual victim, eaten as a sacrifice. The superhuman mother, or goddess, was eaten typically or by proxy. Hence she who was the giver of food and life to the world came to be eaten sacramentally and vicariously, that is, in some Totemic victim, by whose death her sacrifice was symbolically represented. There were different types of the sacrificial victim at different stages of the eucharist. At one stage it was the Red Calf as the type of Horus, the Child; this same type was continued in the Hebrew ritual, it was carried on under various types in different Cults, and finally into the Christian doctrines.

Whilst some of these Nilotic Negroes carried out the primitive wisdom from the same central birthplace in Africa (at the head of the Nile and around the Great Lakes) to the islands of the Southern Seas and other places, and were fossilized during long ages of isolation, those that remained carried it down the Nile to take living root and grow, develop, flourish and expand as the mythology and Eschatology of Ancient Egypt : as an example, "the Mysteries of Amenta" are more or less extant in the Totemic ceremonies of the Central Australians, Arunta tribes at a rudimentary stage of development, which means, according to the present reading of the data, "that they have retained the true origin."

In the Mysteries of Amenta the deceased is reconstructed from seven constituent parts or souls in seven stages of development.

Corresponding to these in the Arunta Mysteries, seven "status-terms" are applied to the initiate : (1) he is called Ambaquerka up to the time of his being tossed in the air ; (2) he is Ylpmerka until taken to the circumcision ground ; (3) he is the Wurtja during the time betwixt being painted for it and the active performance of the ceremony ; (4) he is Arakurta betwixt the operation of circumcision and sub-incision ; (5) he is Ertwa-Kurka after circumcision until he passes through the ordeal of fire ; (6) following this he is called Illpongwurra, and (7) after passing through the

Engwura he is designated Urliara. In the Mysteries of Amenta the mouth of the resuscitated spirit is opened and the silence of death is broken when the lips are touched by the sacred implement in the hands of Ptah. It is said in "the ceremony of opening the mouth," "Let my mouth be opened by Ptah with the instrument of ba-metal, with which he opened the mouth of the gods" (chap. 23). The Arunta also perform the ceremony of opening the mouth by touching it with a sacred object when the initiates are released from the ban of silence. This is still practised by the Roman Christian Church on the death of each Pope.

The first act of initiation in the Arunta Mysteries is that of throwing the boy up into the air. This was a primitive mode of dedication to the ancestral purity of the Totem, or the tribe, whose voice is heard in the sound of the Churinga, or bull-roarer, whirling round. It is said by the natives that the voice of the Great Spirit was heard when the resounding bull-roarer spoke. The Great Spirit was supposed to descend and enter the body of the boy and to make him a man, just as in the Mystery of Tattu the soul of Horus the Adult descends upon and unites with the soul of Horus the Child, or the soul of Ra the Holy Spirit descends upon Osiris to quicken and transform and re-erect the mummy. Where risen Horus becomes bird-headed, as the adult in spirit, the

Arunta youth is given the appearance of flight, to signify the change resulting from the descent of the spirit as the cause of transformation. When one becomes a soul in the Mysteries of the *Ritual* by assuming the form or image of Ra, the initiate exclaims, "Let me wheel round in whirls, let me revolve like the turning one" (chap. 83). The "turning one" is the Sun-god Kheper, whose name is identical with that of an Australian tribe, Chepara (Kheper), as the soul of "self-originating force," which was imaged under one type by the Bennu, a bird that ascends the air and flies to a great height whilst circling round and round in spiral wheels (*Ritual*, chap. 85). Whether this be the Churinga, the Bribbun, Turndun or whirler in a glorified form or not, the doctrine of soul-making at puberty is the same in the Australian as in the Egyptian Mysteries. In the Egyptian mythology Horus is the blind man, or rather he is the child born blind, called Horus in the Dark. He is also described as the Blind Horus in the city of the blind. In his blindness he is typical of the emasculated sun in winter and of the human soul in death. A part of this is enacted in the 18°. At the place of his resurrection or rebirth there stands a tree, up which he climbs to enter spirit life. In Australia, near to Charlotte Waters, is the tree that rose to mark the spot where a blind man died. This tree is called the Apera Okilchya—that is, the blind man's tree—and the place where it stands was the camp of the blind, the city of the blind, the world of the dead, in which the tree of life or dawn was rooted (*Northern Tribes*, p. 552). Should the tree be cut down, the men where it grows will become blind. They would be like Horus in the Dark, this being the tree of light or the dawn of Eternal Day. In one of their ceremonies the Arunta perform the mysteries of the fight before Horus and the Sebau, in a primitive phase. The *Chepara tribe* of Southern Queensland also perform the greater Mystery of the Kurigal, in which may be identified the baptism and rebirth by fire. It is the same in signification as the Arunta Mysteries of the purification by fire. The same ceremony is described in the *Ritual* as an exceedingly great mystery and a type of the hidden things in the underworld (chap. 137A).

A mystery of the resurrection is acted also by the Arunta in the *Quabarra Ingwuringa inkinga*, or corroboree of the arisen bones, which bones imaged the dead body, whilst the performers represented the Ulthaana, or spirits of the dead. The bones were sacredly preserved by those who were as yet unable to make the mummy as a type of permanence. Every native has to pass through certain ceremonies before he is admitted to the secrets of the tribe. The first takes place about the age of ten or twelve years, whilst the final and most impressive one is not passed through until probably the native has reached the age of at least twenty-five or thirty years. These two initiations thus correspond to, or represent the origin of, those mysteries of the double Horus. At twelve years of age the child Horus makes his transformation into the adult in his baptism or other kindred mysteries. Horus as the man of thirty years is initiated in the final mystery of the resurrection. So was it with the gnostic Jesus. The long lock of Horus, the sign of childhood, was worn by him until he attained the age of twelve years, when he was changed into a man.

With the Southern Arunta tribe the hair of the boy is for the first time tied up at the commencement of the opening ceremony of the series by which he is made a man. His long hair is equivalent to the Horus Lock. The most sacred ceremonial object of the Arunta is called the Kanana. This is erected at the close of the Engwura mysteries. A young gum-tree, twenty feet in height, is cut down, stripped of its branches and its bark, to be erected in the middle of the sacred ground. The decoration at the top was "just that of a human head." It was covered all over with human blood, unless red ochre had been substituted. The exact significance of the Kanana has been forgotten by the natives—they do not know now. They tell you it has some relation to a human being, and is regarded as common to the members of all the Totems. The mystery is made known at the conclusion of the Engwura series of ceremonies, the last and final of the initiatory rites through which a native must pass before he becomes a fully developed member who is admitted to all the secrets of the tribe.

This is the original of the Egyptian Ka statue, which is a type of eternal duration as an image of the highest soul. To make the Kanana, so to say, the pole is humanized. It is painted with human blood and ornamented like the human head. It has but one form, and is common to all the Totems. So it is with the Egyptian Ka, the eidolon of the enduring soul. The name of the Kanana answers to a long-drawn-out form of the word "Ka" as Kă-ā-ā.

The main difference betwixt the Australian and other Hero and non-Hero Cult natives in various parts of the world and the Egyptian Mysteries is that the one is performed on this earth in the Totemic stage of sociology, the other in the earth of Amenta in the phase of Eschatology, and it is in this latter phase that the "Greater Mysteries" have been handed down to us and left by the Solar Cult people, to whatever country they travelled. Also the Egyptians continued growing all the time that the Nilotic Negroes were standing still or retrograding. Lastly, we may be sure that such mysteries as these did not spring from a hundred different origins and come together by fortuitous concourse from the ends of the earth to be finally formulated as the Egyptian Mysteries of Amenta.

CHAPTER VI

STELLAR CULT PEOPLE AND ORIGIN OF OTHER SIGNS AND SYMBOLS—THE SEVEN LESSER MYSTERIES — THE INITIATORY CEREMONY—WRITTEN LANGUAGE—ANCIENT HITTITE INSCRIPTION TRANSLATED — ORIGIN OF THE OPERATIVE AND SPECULATIVE MASONS AND DIFFERENCES

SIGN LANGUAGE had so developed that the Stellar Cult people converted their signs and symbols into the Ideographic Hieroglyphics and *so formed the first written language.* The signs and symbols they had previously used to express things and mental pictures now became the primary Ideograph of the first written language. The Egyptian Hieroglyphics show us the connection betwixt words and things, also betwixt sounds and words, in a very primitive range of human thought. There is no other such record known in all the world. The government, which hitherto had been pure Socialism, was also carried to a higher state of evolution, and personal possession became predominant and individualistic. National and municipal control, where all was for all, had ceased, and the heads of the government were elected by the people to carry out new laws, established for the good of the community. They first formed two kingdoms under the King of the North and the King of the South; ultimately these were merged into one great kingdom.

They had observed and studied the laws of nature, and founded a code of laws, as a result, that no nation has ever improved upon since. Here is one great lesson for the human race—i.e. Socialism and Bureaucracy cannot be set up in any country now without the destruction of that country following it.

T.G.A.O.T.U. will not allow such a retrograde movement; it is against His Periodic Laws, which He has established, and these are immutable, and any and every nation which attempts it will always be destroyed, as they have many times, the poor ignorant humanity having been set back to a dark and degenerate age, to commence again to climb the Ladder of Light. It will be forever the same in any country where the ignorant are put in office and allowed to try this primitive form of government. These old ancestors of ours had passed the stage of Totemic Sociology or Socialism, never to return to it and live.

The Stellar Cult people now commenced to build cities and develop a very high degree of culture.

The signs, symbols, and Totems of the mythology were divinized into and represented their gods and goddesses in their *astro*-mythology, and became the emblems of the attributes of the One Great God.

This is the reason why it is difficult sometimes to distinguish between Totems and tribes, representing the mothers of the tribes and the Totems, or emblems representing the divinized superhuman Powers, as the same Totem or sign was sometimes used for or represented each.

Many people have stigmatized these people as worshippers of cats, dogs and idols, etc., and still believe it, whereas they were no more *worshippers* of these than the present-day Christians are of the eagle and lamb, which are often seen in Christian churches as symbols of the Divinity. If a sign or symbol represents the Great God, it is not the sign or symbol they worship, but *the Great God.*

The animals were first recognized as Powers in themselves, but they were also adopted as the living visible symbols of Elemental Powers that were superior to the human, as a means of representing natural phenomena. They were further adopted into the human family as Totemic types, with religious rites that gave them all the sanctity of the blood-covenant and made them typically of one flesh with the human brothers. The life-tie assumed between Totemic man and the Totemic animal, or Zootype, was *consciously assumed*, and we thus see on what ground the assumption was made, and the cause of a mystical relationship that was recognized between man and the animals.

It would take too long to give all the details and proofs of their progressive evolution during the 300,000 years which is about the period of time they existed, as far as my researches prove by the finding of their osteo-anatomy and implements in various strata of the earth and rocks.

The Great Pyramid was built by these Stellar Cult people, which proves to what a high degree of knowledge they had attained astronomically and mathematically—a knowledge which has not been equalled by our present astronomers and mathematicians. This is the greatest Masonic Temple that has ever been built, and is emblematical of their mysteries, is astronomically depicted, and therefore belongs to "the seven Primary Mysteries" (see *Arcana of Freemasonry* and *Signs and Symbols of Primordial Man*). There is a statement that they had worked out all their astronomy for 40,000 years before they gave it to the rest of the world, also a statement on parchment found under the corner stone of one of these temples in the Great Foundation in Dendera, in the 4th Dynasty, that "the Great Pyramid was built by the followers of Horus," and these Stellar Cult people were the followers of Horus, just as the Christians are the followers of Christ; indeed, the traditional history is identical almost in every particular, including the Crucifixion.

They sent out colonies all over the world, or nearly all over the world; the exceptions are Australia, New Zealand, and North and South America, where I have so far been unable to find any traces of their remains. Of course, they may have gone there and all traces have been obliterated by the many glacial epochs, which occur roughly about every 26,000 years; but against this we find in these places the descendants of the Nilotic Negro still existing, and apparently they have never been driven away by the Stellar Cult people, as we find in other countries. We can always distinguish them by the remains of their characteristic old temples and osteo-anatomy —not only in Africa, but in Europe, Asia, Central and South America and some of the Pacific Isles. They built their temples with huge polygonal stones and the finest cement. But the principal distinguishing characteristic was that their Great God and all His attributes were portrayed by *iconographic pictures*, i.e. *Zootypes*. These depict not only the Great God and all His attributes, but also the Elemental Powers. By many ignorant people these have been called "idols," because they have not understood, and do not yet understand, the gnosis of their religious ideas and symbolisms, which was always portrayed in Sign Language. The human type was not portrayed as human until *after* the *Stellar Cult. In the Solar Cult temples the human type is depicted in the Stellar Cult Zootypes.*

The exoteric explanation given by various Professors and books hitherto published is not always the true esoteric representation, and this can only be fully understood by following and studying the origin and evolution of the human race and their Sign Language. It is to these old Stellar Cult priests that we owe the origin of our Brotherhood and the *Lesser Mysteries*—the old Her-Seshta, or Wise Men of Egypt, self-designated "the Urshi."

They were the first to cause the primary temple to be built in Egypt, at Edfu. For their sacred buildings they initiated a certain clan, or tribe of men, called the Ari, of the seventeenth Nome of Upper Egypt, *who were the original Operative Masons.*

These builders were initiated into the *first and second Mysteries only,* so that they should keep the secrets of the temples, and no others were ever allowed to build or repair their temples. The Lesser Mysteries were at first seven, but only two of these were ever known to the Operative Masons, past or present. There were two classes of these operatives, called by the priests the Artizans and the Companions. The Operative Masons have divided the first and second Mysteries into four each in recent years, the Blue and the

Red. The first four "work with their hands" —they are operatives of all kinds, the artizans that are required in building. The second four work "with their heads"—the architects, the old original Companions, who draw the plans of the buildings, etc., and see them perfectly carried out. The Operative sacred signs and symbols were given to them as a guide for this knowledge —how to form and build with various angles, circles and other figures, by which the Architects could, by crossing in various ways and positions, portray accurately the plans for the buildings of the old High Priests (see *Arcana of Freemasonry*, chap. xii, for further details). They were unacquainted with, and not informed of, the esoteric meaning of these signs and symbols.

When an exodus, or colony, was sent out from Egypt—and we have it on record that they sent colonies all over the world—a company of these Ari was sent with them, accompanied by a priest who was fully initiated into all the Mysteries. At the present day the Operatives still have their priest attached to their Lodge—he is never initiated in the Operative Lodge, but by a Priest's Lodge.

When he enters a new Lodge, none of the W.'s or D.'s have anything to do with him. Jachins of the Priest's Lodge lead him to one of the Three Masters, who gives him a "password" enabling him to enter that Lodge at any time, and then conducts him to his position in that Lodge. He is never prepared as an apprentice and does not receive a "bond," never pays any fees, and *the ceremony of his initiation is unknown to the Operatives.*

He has a special sign which *no other member of the Operative Lodge* dares to give.

He is the representative of the old High Priest who accompanied the first and other exodes of the Ari from Egypt, and who were the builders of all the great Stellar temples that we find scattered over many lands of the world.

The whole of the Rites and Ceremonies of the Operative Masons should be the first and second Stellar Cult of the "Lesser Mysteries," but I find much innovation has been made in later years by the introduction of "Solar positions," which may be accounted for, because these "Ari," after the Stellar Cult, built for the Solar Cult people in many parts of the world. These Operatives spread throughout the world wherever the Stellar Cult people settled, and afterwards with the Solar Cult people. They were no doubt the originals of all those Operative Guilds we find throughout Europe in later times, some of whom established themselves first at Rome and then in many parts of Europe, during the dark and degenerate Middle Ages, and finally in these Isles, where they ultimately formed the Operative Lodges of Masons. The so-called "Speculative Masons" of the present day, however, *never originated from these*, as some Brothers suppose. In fact, about 600,000 years ago *these Operatives were initiated into the first and second Mysteries by the Her-Seshta, who were the originals of the so-called "Speculatives."*

What I have written is critical proof of my contention, and there are many other proofs, if required. In this book there will not be space enough to give all.

Our Brotherhood, i.e. the so-called Speculative Masons, originated with the old Stellar Cult Her-Seshta priests, who instituted the seven primary Egyptian Mysteries—called the Lesser Mysteries—and these were founded on their astro-mythology, the original mould being supplied by the Totemic Mysteries of the more primitive man, the Hero-Cult Totemic people and their dawning mythology. The Mysteries were a dramatic mode of communicating the secrets of primitive knowledge in Sign Language, which now had become extended to the astronomical mythology, and to teach the doctrines of final things.

Later, during the Solar Cult, ten more Mysteries were added, which were Eschatological and were called the Greater Mysteries, or the "Mysteries of Amenta." The difference between these is that the primary are the Mysteries of Time, the others the Mysteries of Eternity.

The Greater Mysteries were ten in number at first; later, two more were added.

The Lesser Mysteries in their origin were partially Sociological. They were the customs and the ceremonial rites of Totemism.

The Greater are Eschatological and religious. For instance, the transformation of the youth into the adult, or the girl into a woman, in the Totemic Mysteries was applied doctrinally to the transformation of the soul in the Mysteries of Amenta.

With the primitive races the Mysteries remain chiefly Totemic and Sociological, though interspersed with religious sentiment.

The Greater Mysteries were perfected in the Egyptian religion, to be read in the *Ritual* as "The Mysteries of Amenta."

The mythological representation was first applied to the phenomena of external nature, and the mode or representation was continued and re-applied to the human soul in the Eschatology. Many of our signs and symbols connected with the Mysteries and originating with the old Stellar Cult priests I will set forth here, but there are many more which we do not now use; these have been lost to the "Craft," although I am well acquainted with them and their symbology.

I will first portray how the little Pygmy's sacred sign and the Nilotic Negroes were brought on into this Stellar Cult.

The Sacred Axe  (called in Egyptian *Neter*) was brought on in this Cult as a representative symbol for the Great One; and in their temples —the first of which were circular and afterwards built in the form of a double square; at first two cubes, and later three cubes—were always placed in the centre of the Temple; on each of these cubes was engraved the Sacred Axe  or  as a sign and symbol for the Great One. The first represented Horus, God of the North, the second Set, the God of the South, and the third, in the centre, Shu, the God of the Equinox. This formed the Primary Trinity. These were the three primary children out of seven of the old Earth Mother, now divinized as Apt in the astro-mythology, as Gods of the North and South Poles and Equinox. This was also depicted by an equilateral triangle placed on the upper cube with the three names at the three different corners and surrounded by a circle.

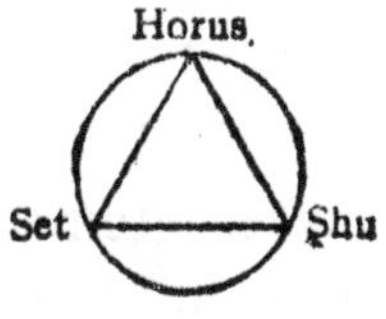

We have no cube, or double or treble cubes in the centre of our Lodges, but the Irish Brothers have retained the original. Also the R.A. Lodges have for their three G.O.'s.

Another form of the original Pygmy sign was its conversion into a simple cross—which was an ideographic symbol for Amsu, or the Risen Horus, or Risen Christ, of the Egyptians. It is the same form or symbol as used by our Red Cross, so familiar to-day =Amsu, the Stellar ideographic symbol for the Risen Horus.

The two poles or pillars , used by the Nilotic Negroes in their ceremonies to represent the North and South divisions of heaven and the North and South Pole Stars, were now brought on in the Stellar Cult as the representative symbols for Set, God of the South, and Horus, God of the North, and were called the Set and Horus Pillars, and were erected at the porchway entrance of every temple (see *Ritual*), the same as we find stated *re* traditional Temple of K.S.; in fact, no temples were ever built without them during the Stellar or Solar Cults.

Josephus has preserved a tradition concerning two pillars that were erected in the land of Siriad. He tells us that the children of Seth (Egyptian Set) were the inventors of astronomy, and in order that their inventions might not be lost, and acting upon Adam's prediction that the world was to be destroyed at one time by the force of fire, and at another time by the violence and quantity of waters, they made two pillars, the one of brick, the other of stone; they inscribed their discoveries upon them both, that in case the pillar of brick should be destroyed by the flood, the pillar of stone might remain and exhibit those discoveries to mankind, and *also inform them that there was another pillar of brick erected by them.* "Now this remains in the land of Siriad to this day" (*Ant.*, B. I, chap. ii). Plato likewise speaks of these two columns in the opening of *Timæus.* The place where the two pillars, or one of them, traditionally stood was in the land of Siriad. Where that is, no mortal man knows. But Seri in Egyptian is a name for the South. Seri is also the mount that is figured as the twofold rock, which is equivalent to the two pillars of the two horizons, South and North. Seri is also the name of the giraffe, a Zootype of Set, the overseer. Siriad, then, is the land of the South, where the pillar "remains to this day." According to John Greaves, the old Oxford astronomer, these pillars of Seth were in the very same place where Manetho placed the pillars of Taht, called Seiread (*English Weights and Measures*). It is possible to identify the missing pillar of the two, the pillar of Set in the South. There was a Southern Annu and a Northern Annu in Egypt, and possibly a relic of the two poles may be recognized in the two Annus, viz. Hermonthes, the

Annu of the South, and Heliopolis, the Annu of the North, the original meaning of Annu being the place or pillar or stone that marked the foundation which preceded the ⊕ sign of station or dwelling-place.

There was an Egyptian tradition which connected Set, the inventor of astronomy, with Annu, as the original founder of the pillar which makes him the primary establisher of the Pole. As an astronomical character Set was earlier than Shu. The Arabs also have a tradition that one of the pyramids was the burial-place of Set. The pillar of brick, being less permanent, went down, as predicted, in the deluge as a figure of the Southern Pole, whereas the pillar of stone remained forever as an image of the North Celestial Pole, or of Annu, the site of the pillar, in the astronomical mythology. It is reported by Diodorus that Annu (Heliopolis in the Solar Mythos) was accounted by its inhabitants to be the oldest city in Egypt, which may have been mystically meant, as Annu was also a city or station of the Pole, the most ancient foundation in the northern heaven, described in the Eschatology as the place of a thousand fortresses provisioned for eternity. The two pillars, therefore, of Set and Horus were primal as pillars of the two Poles thus figured in the equatorial regions as the two supports of heaven, when it was first divided into two portions,

South and North, and the pillar or mount of the South was given to Set, the pillar or mount of the North to Horus. The typical two pillars are identified with and *as* Set and Horus in the inscription of Shabaka from Memphis, in which it is said: "The two pillars of the gateway of the House of Ptah are Horus and Set."

Added to the first form (*supra*) four lines were now drawn across the top to represent the Heavens as a Square and the Earth as a Square, and were called in Egyptian Tatt and Tattu. The word Tattu denotes the two Tatt pillars. Tatt is a figure of stability and supports the four corners, and is therefore equal to a square.

Thus the two Tatt pillars at the entrance  are equivalent to a double square. Tatt is the entrance or gateway to the region where the Mortal Spirit is blended with the Immortal Spirit, and thereby established for ever. In a later form the globes replaced the square , one representing the celestial and the other the terrestrial world. Of other important signs and symbols which we use, originating in this Cult, the first was the triangle of Set  =an ideographic symbol for Set, God of the South, and this triangle  followed, which is an ideographic symbol for Horus, God of the North. This latter symbol is still used by Brothers of the 33°.

The equilateral triangle represents the sacred number three, first as the perfect number, secondly as a symbol of the One Great Triune God, and thirdly as the symbol of the three divisions of heaven, which followed the two divisions of North and South by adding the centre as represented by Shu.

Amongst the Hindus the equilateral triangle is called "Aum," which is the same as the Egyptian Atum, the Great God of the Infinite and of All Things, the Everlasting One, and this has been brought on in our symbolism as the triangle with the All-seeing Eye under the name of T.G.A.O.T.U.

Another form was  representing Horus, God of the North, and Set, God of the South, as the two brothers at the Equinox or Equator, called in Egyptian Apta, or the highest land, because here the two Pole Stars were equally visible. They also doubled this symbol and surrounded it by four Uræi; it then was an ideographic symbol for the Khiu Land, or the Land of the Spirits. When Horus became Primary Deity they were merged into one as  (called the five-pointed star), representing Horus as God of the North and South. It was also an ideograph for the celestial world, or House of Horus, i.e. Paradise.

The circle  also originated with these old Stellar Cult people, representing Heaven as a circle and the Earth as a circle ; it also represented an emblem of Eternity and the ● in the centre of the circle 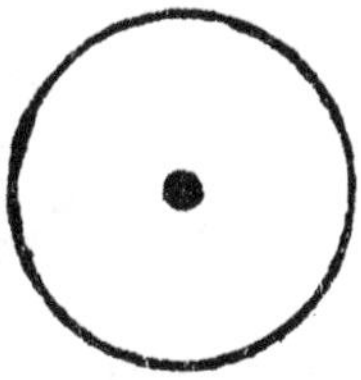 represented the All-seeing Eye of the Great One, and equals the ● or star at the summit of the cone . Another symbol was that of a coiled serpent with its tail in its mouth, forming a circle, as an emblem of eternity. All the primary temples were built in a circular form. This can be seen to-day amongst the descendants of an early exodus—namely, the Chinese, Koreans, and old Japanese, who are all Stellar Cult people, and that is the reason we find so many signs and symbols identically the same as we use amongst them—the signs and symbols of the Stellar Cult Lesser Mysteries. But of late years some of the Solar Cult people and their doctrines have migrated into these countries and so corrupted the pure Stellar Cult.

In these isles and many other countries we find remains of old temples in the form of two circles—one North and one South—which can always be distinguished from the Solar because these

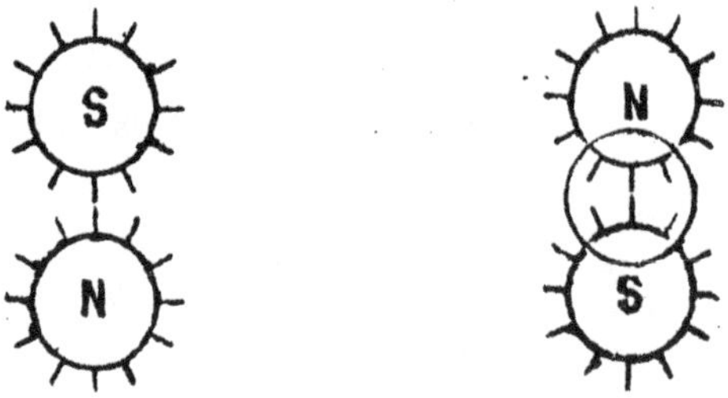

latter are built with three circles, one North, one South, and a third bisecting these in the centre, proving that both of these people existed in these islands long ago. The former represents heaven as twelve divisions in the North and twelve divisions in the South, a pre-zodiacal portrayal, and the Solar added twelve divisions in the centre, making the thirty-six zodiacal divisions. Stellar temples were first oriented South, later North, the Solar always East. Although the Stellar Cult people formed and founded many great nations throughout the world, they never advanced to a higher type anatomically outside Egypt, but always remained the same as at the time of their exodus. This can be proved by their osteo-anatomy and their remains found all over the world where they travelled.

The square  was also founded by these Stellar Cult people (Egyptian name is *Neka*), and it was used in two senses amongst the Ancient Brotherhood, as we use it. That is, it was used by the Operatives to square the stones of the buildings and by the Urshi in a moral sense. It was the seat of judgment and the foundation of Eternal Law in the Court of Divine Judgment, and to build on the square signifies to build on the fourfold foundation for eternity.

All the Stellar Cult people wrote in "glyphs," but their original hieroglyphics became altered in process of time *outside* Egypt, on account of the crude material they used, and their stylos were not so perfect; but to one who has followed them from their old home the transition states are not very difficult to read and understand, even when there is very little of the original left. As an example, I give you my decipherment of a Hittite inscription, the translation of which was unknown until I published it.

AN ANCIENT HITTITE INSCRIPTION.

A Chronicle of the Period.

Photographic reproduction of original.

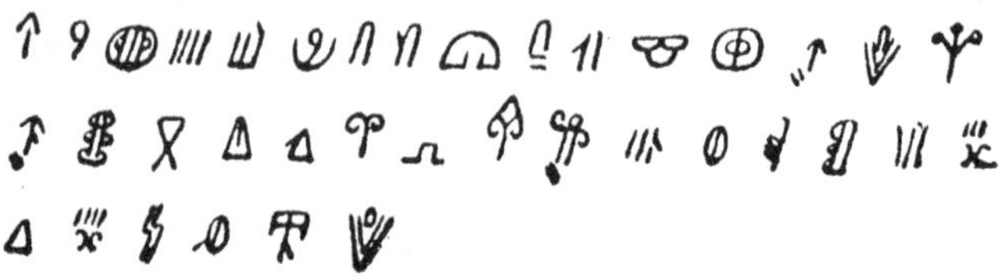

In the modern idiom it reads as follows:

"The (Great) Chief of the Festivals made great offerings to purify the Temple and caused to be opened, or raised up again, twelve chambers of the Temple. The two great Sem Priests of Hait have caused an enclosure, or wall, to be built and have made great libations of flesh and blood to purify this Temple of Horus, God of the North and South. They rejoiced and set up proclamation and caused gifts of food to be carried to the Holy Places of the Temple, and did not refuse Princes, strangers to the country, who wished to speak and rejoice and go before the buildings in the field to wash and to purify and make offerings of flesh and blood, and see the Holy Temple of the great Sem Priest of the Lord."

The importance and great interest attached to this inscription is the symbol of Horus[1] , God

[1] It is a primary form of the five-pointed star.

of the North and the South, as seen portrayed here, which proves conclusively that it was written during the Stellar Mythos, therefore before the Lunar or Solar, and before Menes, the supposed king of the supposed 1st Dynasty. The characters are the old Egyptian hieroglyphics, showing the alteration of the original ideographic and syllabic characters which had taken place after an exodus had left Egypt. All the exodes who left Egypt and went to the East travelled through Asia and then across America (Mexico and South America), and retained the original hieroglyphic writings; but the characters became altered by time and through being written by blunter stylos and on cruder material than the Egyptians used, so that ultimately there was very little of the original glyphs depicted. All the later exodes (Solar) that went up through the Mediterranean and Europe carried out with them the linear alphabetical writings which Professor Evans has named proto-Egyptian, which writings prove that the old Egyptians had already commenced an alphabet, which terminated in their Hieratic and Demotic script, and finally these were altered by time and circumstances into our present-day writings.[1]

[1] For an example of this form of writing see *Arcana of Freemasonry*, p. 224. I have given there a reproduction of the transition stage of writing on ivory tablets found in the Tomb of Naquada, now in the British Museum, and a translation literally and ideographically of the same, never before translated into English.

The Cable T., the Hood, the O. and I.G. implements of office and the 24-inch gauge, which was the original old cubic measure, were all founded by these old Stellar "Urshi."

The 24-inch gauge, or old cubit, is an ideographic hieroglyphic, and has the phonetic value of Maat, and indicated that which is straight, and was the name given to the instrument by which the work of the "Craftsman" was kept straight and measured.

There is also an esoteric meaning—a rule or law, a canon by which the lives of men and their actions were kept straight and governed. The Ancient Brothers used the word in a physical and moral sense as we do, as their naming it Maat clearly proves.

Our Blazing Star, or "The Bright Morning Star," was the Egyptian "Sothos," and is first shown in Zootype form as Anubis, who guided the souls through the underworld; in another type it represents Horus of the Resurrection. In the *Ritual* it states:

"It was the Star of Horus, and his guide, which led him to Paradise, where he seated himself upon the Throne; and *then Horus gave his Star as a guide to his followers.*" In one representation in the Egyptian he is seen with the Star on his head, beckoning to his followers. This is one proof that our present *Ritual* originated from the old Stellar Cult Lesser Mysteries, and has been brought down by the Brotherhood through ages of time to the present day.

The stars were used by the Egyptians to form uranographic pictures on the canvas of the heavens that were imperishable, to illustrate the Mysteries that were unvisualized. The old Urshi, knowing that if the secrets were written on books of stone or papyri, in time these must perish, but as depicted and portrayed, the secret gnosis of the Mysteries would be handed on from generation to generation until time on Earth would be no more, thus wrote in Sign Language, unintelligible to the ignorant masses, who would have destroyed other forms of record, but would leave these, which were of "no value" to them, because they could not read or understand their symbolism; which records were, however, to be read and translated by future generations, for a guidance to posterity of that everlasting truth given by God to man. That divine revelation, which has passed through so many phases and is now preached as the Christian doctrines (without the dogmas), was first promulgated to these Stellar Cult people, and we Freemasons still continue it, in its purest form. If all the Churches of every denomination recognized knew, and preached the Truth, we should have a pure religion which all would believe in, and a higher, nobler and better type of the human would be evolved, with the result that the brotherhood of man would be more firmly cemented together than by any other means.

There are many other signs and symbols which I have given in *Arcana of Freemasonry* and *Signs and Symbols of Primordial Man*, with full explanations, and which I need not repeat here, as it would occupy too much space and time. The Brothers cannot fail to see and understand why we find so many signs and symbols in various parts of the world, and why the present-day Stellar people still use them in their religious ceremonies. They will only find the *Lesser Mysteries* amongst the *true Stellar Cult* people; and when we find the symbols of the Greater Mysteries we know that Solar Cult has crept in, and later the Christian. But the old Stellar Cult Mysteries have never ceased to be practised even up to the present day, as may be seen in some parts of Asia—amongst the Yezidies in the mountains of Mosul, for example—and in some parts of South America.

The initiatory ceremonies in the Lesser Mysteries were conducted with the greatest secrecy and care, as they were also in the Greater. The Candidates were divested of most of their clothing and a chain or rope placed around their neck, to signify their belief in God, their dependence on Him, and their solemn obligation to submit and devote themselves to His Will and service.

The fact that they were neither naked nor

clothed was an emblem that they were untutored men, children of nature, unregenerated and destitute of any knowledge of the true God, as well as being destitute of the comforts of life.

The chain or rope was a symbol that signified that the Candidate was being led from darkness to light, from ignorance to knowledge of the One True Living God, Creator and Judge of all things in Heaven and on Earth. The Candidate had a hood or thick veil placed over his eyes, so that he could not see, and was led by a Brother, called in Egyptian *An-er-f*, to the door of the Temple or Lodge, which appeared as a blank wall. At the door or entrance was a "Watcher" armed, who said to the Candidate, "I will not open to thee," "I allow thee not to pass by me unless thou tellest me my name." The word was "Shu-Si-Ra." (The answer, translated from the Egyptian, was "The Kneeler," i.e. Shu.) He was then given a password, which in Egyptian is "Ra-gririt"—"The door of stone." The door was an equilateral triangle, a symbol typical of Heaven, and a square stone underneath on which he trod was a symbol typical of Earth. The whole symbolized passing from Earth to Heaven. He was then conducted through long passages, through difficulties, danger and darkness, and around the Lodge seven times; during this he had to answer various questions, words of power and might being given him. Finally he was conducted to the centre of the Lodge. He was asked what he desired most. His answer was that Light might be given him. Thoth, the recorder of Truth, then removed the veil of darkness, and he was invited to join and unite in the circle and feast. If the Candidate turned back or violated his obligations, his throat was cut and his head chopped off, after his heart had been torn out (see *Ritual*, chaps. 27, 28, 40, and 90).

The W.M. or High Priest was placed in his chair with the same grip and token as we use at the present day, except that it was the other arm and the word was "Maat-Heru," meaning "One whose voice must be obeyed." The present is a substituted one, the meaning of which correctly is "Stone squares."

The Jewel representing the forty-seven Problems of the First Book of Euclid worn by the Master has no meaning, as it is explained to him. With the old Brotherhood the correct meaning of it was the triangle of Horus, and the three squares represented the three Grand or Great Originals of the Primary Trinity. With the Operative Masons the three squares represent the first, second, and third Masters of the Lodge.

CHAPTER VII

THE LUNAR CULT—THE SOLAR CULT—ORIGIN OF OTHER SIGNS AND SYMBOLS—ORIGIN OF THE TEN GREATER MYSTERIES, OR MYSTERIES OF AMENTA—THEIR PERVERSION BY THE GREEKS AND OTHER NATIONS

AFTER the Stellar came the Lunar Cult, so called because they reckoned their time by the moon instead of the stars. Not much evidence exists, that I have been able to discover, of many of our signs and symbols having originated amongst the Lunar Cult people. They carried on and made use of all the signs and symbols of the old Stellar people, only using different terminology for the names of the divinized Elemental Powers.

In the Lunar Cult, which followed the Stellar, before the Solar, we find man first tried to portray the human figure. The proof of this is in the many "finds," both in Egypt and along the Mediterranean Basin and also in Brazil, where the Lunar Cult people travelled after they had left Egypt and after the Stellar Cult people ceased to exist there. The majority of the remains found are those of *part of a female*, or child, only, never the complete human figure. *And parts of these female figures are characteristic of the female Pygmy.*

In the Egyptian Museum at Turin there are

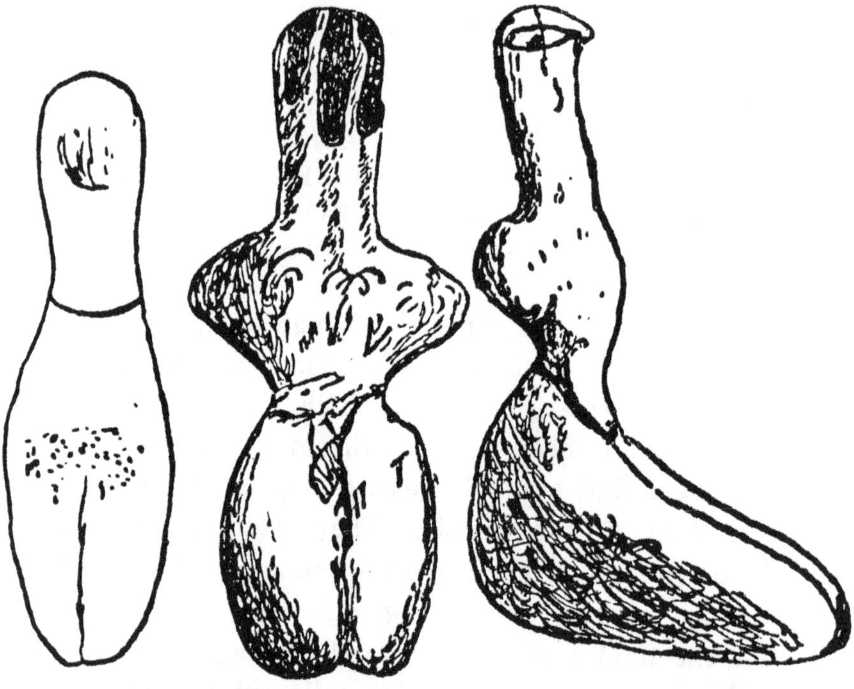

Early Egyptian figures of unbaked clay, with decorations of animal figures (Zootypes); date, late Lunar or early Solar. Similar are found throughout the Mediterranean Basin, Europe, Brazil, and other parts of the world where the Lunar Cult-people migrated. The types are taken from the Pygmy women to represent the Great Mother, and this was prior to the Pygmy-man Ptah.

five female figures bought at Luxor by Professor Ernesto Schiaparelli, and the Professor is convinced that these figures are prior in date to the

1st Dynasty. Undoubtedly he is right in his opinion.

They are statuettes formed by the late Lunar Cult people, or very early Solar, long before the 1st Dynasty.

I give some drawings here to show the first attempts to depict the Mother-goddess in human form—because it was the Mother that was first depicted and not the Father; the Father was not symbolized before the Solar Cult. The Great Mother had been portrayed in Zootype forms[1] from the first Stellar Cult, as a Tree, or Cow, or Sow, or Hippopotamus, but now in the later part of the Lunar Cult there is an attempt to depict the Great Mother in human form.

There are two types of this portrayal that we find all over the world where the Lunar Cult people travelled—Europe, some parts of Asia, and South America, as well as throughout Africa—and both these types were taken from the Pygmies. One is steatopygous, the other not, and I found these two types amongst the Pygmies living at the present time. This is a further proof that the Egyptians knew and recognized the Pygmies as the first living humans, and tried to portray them even before they did Bes-Horus, during the early Solar Cult. These are not Bushman or Hottentot women, because their anatomical differences prove this. With the Bushman and Hottentot women

[1] See *Origin and Evolution of the Human Race.*

the *labia minora* have so extreme a development that they hang down to the length of 15 centimetres.[1] This is not present in any of these first figures of the human race, nor is it present in any of the Pygmy races wherever you may find them, thus proving my contention that the old Egyptians first depicted the human form as a type taken from the Pygmy, because they knew that the Pygmy was the first human evolved, and that the first depiction was the female type, a "mother." The figures found were intended to represent Hathor, the Moon-goddess, and her child Horus—the Great Mother, earlier symbolized as a Cow with her child, Horus, as a Calf or Bull.

The finding of so many of these figures and bulls' heads at Phæstos proves that the Minoan and Mycenæan civilizations were principally during the Lunar and first Solar Cults, and, therefore, comparatively late in Egyptian history, as the Stellar Cult had undoubtedly existed in Egypt for 300,000 years before the Lunar and first Solar. The Cult of the Great Mother and Child was thus brought on from the Stellar to the Lunar Cult. No doubt, however, there was some overlapping of the Cults during the Minoan and Mycenæan civilizations—but the civilization was not prior to the Egyptian, as many Professors state and believe; what I have written is quite sufficient proof against such a statement.

1. See *Origin and Evolution of the Human Race.*

The Mycenæan symbolism of the two lions with the central tree, or the pillar, can be read if followed as Egyptian, but not otherwise. The tree, the pillar, or the mount was female, as a figure of the birthplace, the place of exit for the babe born from the mount, the Meskhen, or its equivalent in Sign Language. She was the House of Horus, and the House was imaged as a cone or tree, or some other type, and this will explain why the Mycenæan figure accompanying the tree-pillar is at times a woman and at other times a child. They are the goddess and her babe, identical with Hathor and the child Horus in the place of birth.

In the gold shrine found at Mycenæ (Evans, Fig. 65), the figures on each side are two doves. The dove in Egypt was the very ancient bird of Hathor, and the figure on each side is a dove, equivalent to the mother and the child who was born within her shrine, her house, her pillar, or her tree, as the dove of the generative spirit or the later Holy Spirit. The double axe of what has been called "the Mycenæan Tree and Pillar Cult" is an emblem of the double power, and the so-called god of the double axe is consequently a god of the double equinox or double horizon, who in a later form was Har-Makhu, the Horus who passed into Amen-Ra of the Egyptians. Various symbolisms of the Egyptians are found in many parts of the world, which Evans and

Count d'Alviella have given in their writings and books, but the interpretation can always truly and definitely be found by reading the ancient Egyptian Sign Language. Without a fundamental knowledge of the mythology and the Sign Language as framework, it is impossible to comprehend the doctrines of the Egyptian religion. In the Stellar Cult the birthplace was in Sothos. Both the Mother and Child met there, and this star symbolizes the birthplace of Horus in the Stellar Cult.

Following the Lunar came the Solar Cult, so called because these people had found that the time hitherto was not correctly recorded, and so they changed and kept their time by the sun.

The Lunar and Solar people had developed to a much higher type of Homo in evolution in Egypt, as may be seen by their physiognomy and also osteo-anatomy.

They sent out colonies to many parts of the world, and spread over Africa and Europe, some parts of Asia, landed at Yucatan, in America, and went South as far as the Southern portion of Peru, exterminating the Stellar Cult people, or imposing their religious doctrines upon them wherever they were able to do so.

One of the reasons different types originated in various countries and different types in evolution was the intermarriage of these people with the Stellar Cult and other women. (See *Origin and*

Evolution of the Human Race for further details and proof.) The Solar people added ten more Mysteries to the seven previous ones, which they called the *Greater Mysteries.* These are more particularly carried on and practised now by what are called the Higher Degrees under the Supreme Council, but are much mixed up and perverted from the true originals.

It was during the Solar Cult that the human form was fully first portrayed, replacing the Zootypes, depicting the G.G. and all His attributes.

The Stellar and Solar people can also be traced by their form of writing. The Stellar Cult people wrote only in hieroglyphics or glyphs, whereas the Solar people began to form an alphabetical writing, commencing with what Professor Evans has termed Proto-Egyptian, finally developing into the Hieratic and Demotic. An example is shown, with decipherment, on p. 224 of *Arcana of Freemasonry.*

To return again to our little Pygmy's sacred sign for the " Great One " or " Great Chief."

I reproduce here (see next page) a rough drawing the exact size of a Sacred Axe found near Chelsham, Kent, and given to me by Mr. Smith, of the " White Bear," Chelsham. It is composed of hard sandstone.

I know of no other Sacred Axe like this. It is typical and genuine, but I could not say if this belonged to the Stellar Cult or primary Solar people. I think probably the latter.

The Solar people used this in two forms; first, as the Hammer or Axe, the proof being that Ptah at Memphis was called the Great Chief of the Hammer, or the Great Chief of the Axe, and

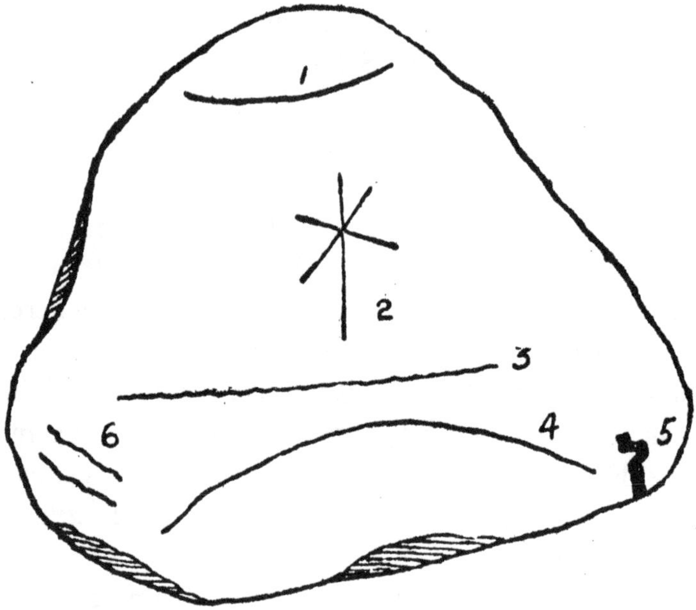

1. Deep cut, ends obliterated.
2. Sign and Symbol of Amsu.
3. Faint line across.
4. Deep cut, ends obliterated.
5. Terminal of one end, but deep marking.
6. Two faint lines.

Shaded portion chipped off.

was symbolically represented as such in one form. In still an earlier Cult, Horus was the Great Chief of the Hammer, a Cleaver of the Way, as Horus of the Double Horizon.

Second, this original Pygmy sacred sign  in the Solar Cult became a symbol and ideographic sign for Amsu, the Risen Horus, and as this  it represents a compound sign,  =He descended, and  =He ascended, and the whole symbol is an ideograph for Atum-Iu, of the first Solar Cult, and was the same as the Samash of the Chaldeans, Babylonians and Assyrians—the Horus of the Double Horizon of Egypt, where his name was Atum-Iu on the Eastern Horizon and Atum-Ra on the Western, and is the same as Ramman, God of the Axe, of the Syrians, Chaldeans and the Solar Cult people of Central and South America.[1]

They also used the symbol  Ru, connected with or attached to the original Pygmy sign in many forms ; these are some, and in these forms they have been brought on into the Christian symbolism.

[1] See *Arcana of Freemasonry*.

This symbol , called the Ru, or fish's mouth, is an ideograph for "An." It was used in Egypt as the symbol which represented the giving birth to water, as the life of the world and the Saviour, who comes as the Water of Life—thus the whole symbol, *supra*, represented the Great Saviour of Life, on whom all must depend. The

1. Set.

two triangles of Set and Horus in this Cult 

2. Horus.

were blended together to form a symbol for Horus of the Double Horizon, thus 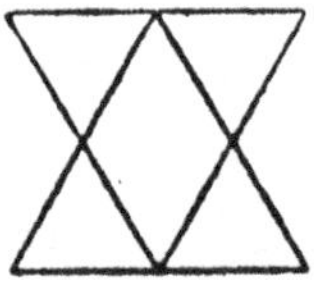, sometimes with a circle round. This is the reason why we find the sign amongst the Druids, Hindus, and Jews of the present day (it is also used by Brothers of the R.A.D.). Their religious Cult is the Primary Solar of the Egyptians. Why it was ever called Solomon's Seal I have never been able to discover, because it was in existence thousands of years before Solomon ever lived, and is an ideograph for Horus of the Double Horizon; other names were Har-Maker, Atum-Huhi, Iu, Aiu, of Egypt. Various forms of all these signs and symbols are found in the British Isles, as well as other parts of the world, on ancient remains, but all originated in Egypt, as I have shown, and were carried forth from there by the many exodes that left that old land. Wherever or in whatever part of the world these are found, and under whatever terminology, we know that the originals were depicted as Sign Language by primitive man, to express his ideas and beliefs in the place of words which he at first did not possess.

CHAPTER VIII

HORUS OF THE DOUBLE HORIZON AND EARLY SOLAR CULTS

HORUS of the Double Horizon was the most profound mystery, and the greatest secret of all the Mysteries established by the old Urshi of Egypt.

It is of the greatest importance to the Brotherhood that they should understand this *in all its phases, on account of the various and many signs and symbols associated with this Cult*, which came into being during the progressive types occurring through a long period of human evolution.

The numerous and different signs and symbols which represent and portray Horus of the Double Horizon and the wide spread of the religious doctrine, found nearly in every part of the world, could never be comprehended and understood without a true knowledge of the evolution which has occurred in past ages of the world's history—the evolution of religious Cults of primitive man, when he spoke and wrote in Sign Language, being unable to express himself in present-day terminology, because he had not then developed the articulate sounds necessary. Thus his ideas and beliefs are all at first expressed in Sign Language; but not less true for that when read correctly.

I therefore explain to the Brotherhood the different types and phases that were employed during the numerous stages of human evolution to express "one and the same belief or doctrine of Horus of the Double Horizon" which has existed from the first to the present day, typified by numerous and different signs and symbols, many of which we still use. This necessarily must be in a condensed form, as the subject, if fully set forth with details of all facts still extant, would fill six large volumes, or more.

(1) The first, the Peseshti, or two halves, that were South and North, representing Set and Horus, were united first and symbolized in the following forms  —the two poles or two pillars for North and South; this was followed by the two circles 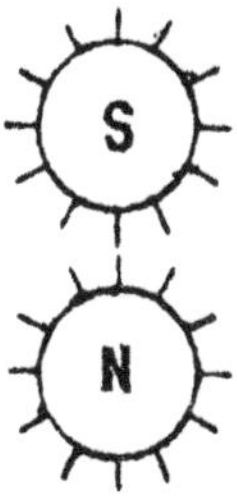

. Then the two triangles,

as 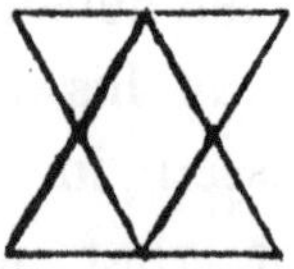 =South and North, or as  as the Horizons of the South and North, and afterwards brought on in the Solar Cult as the

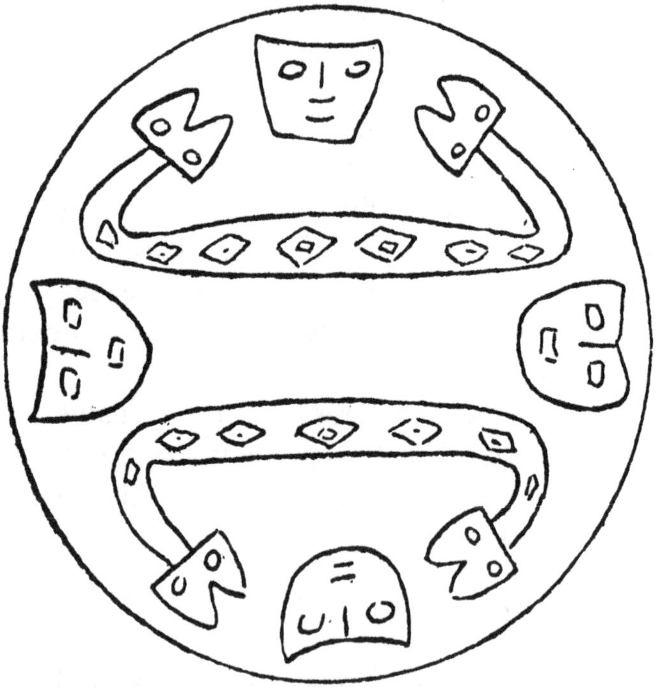

THE NORTHERN AND SOUTHERN DIVISION OF THE HEAVENS.

A Copper Disk from South America, probably from Peru, showing the division of Heaven into North and South, and Shu at the Equator. (*Drawn by K. Watkins.*)

Horizons of West and East, as Horus of the Dual Equinox.

(2) The next portrayal of the "Cult of Horus of

the Double Horizon" was as the so-called "Disk worship," or the Cult of Aten.

The "disk" represented an emblem of the circle made by Aten, as God of both Horizons; and Horus-Behutet, God of the "Hut" or "Winged Disk," was the earliest form of Aten.

The word Aten, from At, was an ancient name for the child who crossed from the horizon West to the horizon East upon the vulture's wings, an emblem of the Motherhood. His was a compound type of godhead, in which the mother was dual with the son, who was her child on one horizon and her "bull or fecundator" on the other.

The "hut" was a dual symbol of the divine infant and the mother as bearer of the child.

As the wings, or bird, she carried him over the intervening void of darkness where the great Apap lay in wait. Thus the godhead of Aten consisted of the mother, her child and the adult male, or "bull of his mother," in the very primary Cult.

Har-Ur, the so-called Elder Horus, is thus represented as the child of the mother when she had no husband; hence she was the Virgin Mother.

The first Horus was also called Horus-Behutet, or "the Great Blacksmith," and was symbolized by the axe or the hammer, "The Cleaver of the Way" (*supra*).

These "wings" (*supra*) are placed in the temples

of the higher degrees; but I am of the opinion that not any of the Brotherhood understand or are acquainted with the true reason, either of their symbolism or why they are placed over the western entrance of our temples. I now have given it them.

The time that this first Cult was developed was when Shu was added to Horus and Set to form the Primary Trinity. Horus and Set were the two gods of the North and South when the divisions of the heavens were dual; then Shu was added at the Equinox to form a tripartite division, or representation, as God of the Centre. In the next phase Horus became supreme as God of the North, South, East and West, and later this primary Cult of Horus of the Double Horizon East and West was instituted.

(3) The next phase of this Cult was represented by Neith, on one Horizon, and Sekhet, on the other, with the child Sebek-Horus, depicted symbolically by the Great Fish, or Crocodile, which was reduplicated as two Crocodiles, to represent the double power or dual horizons.

This is the reason and explanation why we find Horus symbolically represented as a "fish-man," or "by a fish" (see later) in many phases of this Cult. I give here the Christian symbolic representation of the White Vulture of Neith of the

Egyptians as seen in the 18° (sixteenth century).

In the Egyptian representation she is depicted as suckling the two Crocodiles (the Christian is the Pelican feeding her young from her own blood). She was the second representation of the Virgin Mother—both forms were founded during the Stellar Cult and portrayed in Sign Language.

To read this Sign Language correctly we must go back to the time when the autumn Equinox occurred in Virgo—that was the place of conception of Sebak, the fish of the inundation. Six months later the sun rose in the sign of Pisces, and in the eastern Equinox, when the *fish* as child and consort, or as the two Crocodiles, became the two fishes with Neith as the Mother on one horizon and Sekhet on the other. Thus the virgin Neith conceived her child Sebek-Horus, the *fish* of the inundation, which was duplicated to express the adultship, and they were the two typical fishes, or the two Crocodiles. The Crocodile-headed Sebek as the child attributed to Neith in Virgo swims across the waters of darkness, or the abyss of waters, to rise up in the East as Horus of the Twofold Horizon.

This is the reason why we find Horus represented as a " fish man " or by a fish in many phases of Horus of the Double Horizon, the same as the Gnostic Jesus, and also in our present Cult.

I reproduce here a beautiful photograph of Horus standing on two Crocodiles, from Egypt.

He is here symbolized as Horus of the Double or Dual Power or Dual Horizons. The "lock of hair" typifies him as the child of twelve on one Horizon, and the "Head of Bes" shown above signifies him as the man of thirty years on the other.

Thus we perceive how evolution continued as man advanced to a higher plane. First the Pygmies believed in a Supreme or Great Spirit, whom they could not define or comprehend but imaged or symbolized by , which became a representation of the Great Spirit in Sign Language.

In the next phase the Nilotic Negroes, who believed in the same Great Spirit, attributed two primal elemental powers or spirits to Him—Light and Darkness, thus representing or believing Him to be a Dual form, or a Dual God, i.e. God of Light and God of Darkness, as well as God of the North and God of the South, and they imaged this by symbolizing Him as two Birds—one Black, the other White. Later they added the elemental force or spirit of "Breath of Life or Force of Wind," and symbolized or imaged this by a panting or roaring Lion. Thus the Primary Trinity, or a Great Spirit with three attributes of the elemental powers, was first portrayed, imaging Him as God of Darkness, God of Light, and God of the Breath of Life, as well as the God of the North, God of the

The Child Horus on the Crocodiles.

The Egyptian Horus of the Double Equinox or Double Power (see text). (*Drawn by K. Watkins.*)

GILGAMES STRANGLES A LION.[1]

THE SO-CALLED ACCADIAN FIRE GOD.

South, and God of the Centre. In this figure of Horus of the Double Power we find a still further advancement, that is, He is here represented as the God of the Eastern and Western Horizons and a God of the Double Force, as well as the God of the North and South. He is also represented by symbolism as the young Child, representing the Spirit of life in the young Shoot, or the young Fish, or Bird, or Lamb, or other types of "rebirth of Spirit life," also as the adult man, as typified by the head of Bes or Har-Ur, as representing the full development of the Spirit of the Fish, or Shoot, or Tree, or Fruit, or other types. These attributes were the elemental Nature powers or Spirits of Nature, which were visible and cognizant to them, and they objectified the same by this imagery of Symbolism in Sign Language when they had not the terminology to express their ideas and beliefs otherwise.

In no land or literature has the Mythical mode of representation been perverted and reduced to drivelling foolishness more fatally than in some of the Hebrew legends, such as that of Jonah and the great fish, which is connected with the origin of the fish-man in the mythology, who was born of a fish-mother, identifiable with the constellation of the Southern fish and Horus of the inundation, and brought on as types, as Horus of the Double Power. The most ancient type of the fish was female, as a representation of the great Mother-Earth in the water.

This as Egyptian was the Crocodile. She was the suckler of Crocodiles in the inundation. She was the bringer-forth as the great Fish or Crocodile in the Astronomical-Mythology. One of her children was the Crocodile-headed Sebek, who made the passage of the Nun by night, typified as the Child Horus in Solar Mythos. The fish-man was at first the Crocodile of Egypt, next the Crocodile-headed figure of Horus, who is called "the Crocodile God in the form of a man" (*Ritual*, ch. 88).

The conversion of the crocodile god in the Nun to the fish-man of Babylonia was thus made. Jonah is a form of the fish-man in the Babylonian story (which is neither Mythology nor Eschatology), and therefore a figure of both the Stellar and Solar God who made the passage of the waters as Horus the Crocodile, or as Ea the fish-man of Nineveh. Birth or rebirth, from the great fish in the Lower Nun, is one of the oldest traditions of the race. It was represented in the Mysteries and constellated in the heavens as a means of Memorial in Sign Language.

The Astronomical Cult of Egypt passed into Akkad and Babylonia with the exodus of the Stellar Cult race, some of which were termed the Cushite "black-heads"—to become the wisdom of the Chaldees and the Persian Maji in after ages—one of the types.

I produce here a picture of Gilgames, the so-called Fire God of the Accadians.

These people had left Egypt as an exodus during the Stellar Cult, but the earlier Solar was brought into the country by a second exodus, with the old Egyptian Laws up to date, as witnessed by the *stale* of Hammurabi. We see here portrayed Gilgames strangling a lion and serpent—the same as the Egyptian Horus, except that the fauna has been differently portrayed. But the symbolism of the God of the Double Power is the same. They, however, have omitted the two Crocodiles, or two fishes, as the symbolic power for the transmission from the Horizon West to East. The reason was because they had forgotten the old Sign Language, and had converted the Crocodile, which was a type of good and beneficent power in Egypt, into one of bad omen here in Accadia. But the Cult remained the same.

I give on the next page the South American portrayal of Horus of the Double Horizon to prove how widespread this Cult was throughout the world.

The symbolism portrayed here is Horus strangling serpents—one in each hand, signifying the Double Power.

The Egyptian ideograph for the Horizon is in two parts—one on the right, the other on the left, attached to the lower part of the serpents.

The name Iu is shown in Egyptian hieroglyphics attached to his head.

Below we have the representative symbol of the fauna of the country for the Mother-Goddess typified as a bird, with the ideographic Egyptian hieroglyphic for Egypt at the posterior part or base of the head.

This, as in the Lunar symbolism, represents the

This figure was discovered by Professor Uhle on some pottery at Pachacamac, and unmistakably represents the personage on the great monolithic gateway at Tiahuanaco—Horus of the Egyptians, strangling serpents. (*Drawn by K. Watkins.*)

Mother and her child of the Double Power or Double Horizon.

I also give here one of the Mexican portrayals, Horus of the Double Horizon, kneeling with one knee on one Horizon and with his foot put out to tread the other, with the symbol of death and darkness between the two, to show the passage he has to make. Tears are in his eyes ("Ye are the tears," etc.).

His name, Iu, is placed in front of his head, attached to his crown, and is an Egyptian ideograph for his name.

(4) In the next portrayal, which was during the Lunar Cult, also depicted in Sign Language, one of the representations was the Moon-goddess

Hathor, as a Cow, and Horus as her young Calf, as her child on one Horizon and as her Bull on the other (see *supra*).

The passage from West to East was through the Mountain of the West that had been imaged as a passage through the cow of earth.

In the Egyptian Mythos, Tum makes his passage through the Mount by means of the cow and is reborn as Tem, the little child, from the Khepsh of the cow Meh-ur. It is said of him, in setting forth from the Western Horizon, "Earth stretches her arms to receive thee."

He (Tem) is embraced by the Mother, whose womb is the Meskhen of rebirth, and at his coming forth to the Eastern Horizon it is said, "Thou hast rested in the cow, thou hast been immerged in the cow Meh-ur" (inscription of Darin, lines 27–28).

(5) The next portrayal was during the Solar Mythos. In this Solar Cult there were several phases following one upon the other, principally showing how the Fatherhood was substituted for the Motherhood.

Hitherto, from the first inception of religious doctrines, the Matriarchal type had been the first and primary, founded on the Totemic ceremonies of primitive man, originating with Mother Earth, followed by the Mother of the tribe when the Father was not known or not recognized, and astronomically depicted in the Stellar—all symbolized in Zootype forms.

Now, in the Solar Cult, the Fatherhood was recognized and took the place of the Motherhood, as the primary representation and as the first person in human form, although during the first phases of the Mythos the symbolic representation was partially continued.

(6) In the first Solar it was the Cult of Atum-Iu, or Aiu, or Iou, and many other names for the same one.

The representation was Atum-Iu as the child of twelve on one Horizon and Atum-Ra as the Father on the other. This was symbolized by the little autumn sun conceived upon the Western Horizon or Mount, and adultship was attained on the Eastern Horizon with what was termed the double force.

The little sun, or other types, typified the child Horus of twelve years and entered the Western Mount "at the beautiful gate of entrance in the West," for symbolic breeding purposes, and rose again as the great sun, or other types, representing the adult Horus of thirty years, when the godhead consisted of the Mother, the child and the divine adult.

(7) The next form of the Cult was symbolized by the Sphinx.

The Sphinx is a representative image of the god Har-Makhu. We learn from the *Ritual* that the Mystery of the Sphinx originated, or represented, the Mount of Earth, as the place of passage, of burial and rebirth for Horus as the Solar God. It was made as the means of crossing for Horus of the two Horizons or the Double Equinox, and as such was assigned to Atum-Harmachis.

Harmachis entered the Sphinx at sunset in the West or hinderpart, and was reborn in the East as Horus of the fore-part, lion-faced, as representing the double force, the transformer being Kheper. The means of crossing the dark gulf in the Solar Mythos was now the bridge of death, and the mode of uniting the two worlds in one when the re-arising of the sun was succeeded by the resurrection of the soul; the lion having been adopted for the Sphinx upon the Horizon East as an emblem of the double power, the Sphinx being made male in front and female in the hinder-part. It is a compound image of the Mother-Earth and the young god whom she brought forth upon the Horizon of the resurrection. Without the Mother there was no rebirth.

Har-Makhu crossed from one Horizon to the other through the hollow body of the Sphinx, the Sphinx being imaged in a twofold type, with its tail to the West and its head to the East, pointing to the Equinox each way.

The Divine Fatherhood was developed from Har-Makhu, who became the great god Ra in his primordial sovereignty. In this phase we find the double Harmachis, the Sun-god of the Twofold Horizon, who claims a divine origin, or the virgin's child that was not begotten by God the Father. Horus of the Double Horizon was also typified as Horus of the Two Lions. In the *Ritual*, Horus rises again, saying, "I am the twin lions, the heir or Ra" (chap. 38, 1; chap. 62, 2), "I am the double lion" (chap. 72, 9).

(8) The next portrayal comes into view at the time of the supposed 1st Dynasty, when Ptah was the representative of the Great God at Memphis,

and was called the Great Architect of the Universe, but not the universe as a cosmological creation.

Hitherto the stars had been used by the Egyptians to form uranographic pictures on the canvas of the heavens, which was imperishable, to illustrate the Mysteries that were unvisualized.

The old Urshi knew that, if the secrets were written on "Books of Stone," in time these must

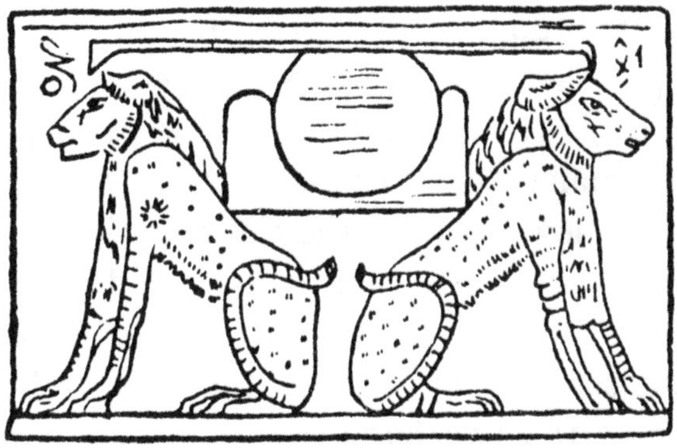

The horizon is seen between the two Lions east and west, representing Horus as the double force. The sun is seen rising between the ideographic horizon, with the ideographic Pet = heaven above. (*Drawn by K. Watkins.*)

The original is in the British Museum. The hieroglyphics read, on the right, *safâ*, "yesterday"; the one on the left, *dûaû*, "this morning."

perish, but as depicted and portrayed, the sacred gnosis of the Mysteries would be handed on from generation to generation, until time on earth would be no more, and so thus wrote them in uranographic Sign Language, unintelligible to the ignorant masses, who would have destroyed other forms of record, but would leave these, which were of no value to them, because they could not read or understand this Sign Language, but which records were to be read and translated by future generations for a guidance to posterity.

Now, Ptah created Amenta with his seven Pygmies or Powers, the hollowing out of the earth as a tunnel for the heavenly bodies and the manes, which were now to make the passage *through* instead of *around* the Mount of Earth. This was not a real tunnel, but a *primitive mode of thinking* through the solid earth—an ideographic representation. It was a lower world through which all the manes had to pass figuratively.

Horus now becomes the Chief of the two Lands and the two Earths, and wears the double diadem as ruler of the double earth, and is now the "traverser of the two earths," as well as the uniter of the two horizons.

The foundation of the Fatherhood was laid when the various powers (now nine in all) were combined in a single Deity to be worshipped as the One True Eternal Spirit.

These were primarily the Great Mother and her seven Elemental Powers. When the goddess was superseded by the god Ptah, both sexes were included in the one Supreme Being, who was now the Lord over all.

Ptah became the god who was born of his own becoming, or of his own self-originating force, who came into existence in the person of his own son as a mode of representing the eternal manifesting in the sphere of time.

The male had been substituted for the Mother as the begetter in matter, symbolized by Kheper as a male beetle, as a type of divine parent as Kheper-Ptah, and the female now became subsidiary to the male. Kheper-Ptah is now called "the Creator of all things that came into being."

Ptah is God the Father in one character and Iu the Son in another.

(9) The Cult that followed this was that of Amen at Annu, where Amen was the one god in the two characters of Father and Iu the Son. In the Cult of Ptah both characters of Father and Son were combined in one god, and so it was in this Cult—the one the Father and the ever-coming son.

(10) The Osirian Cult, the 10°, followed this, and Amenta in one aspect became the world of the dead, the Kasu or burial-place in the Osirian Cult, and Horus the son of Osiris takes the place of Amen or Nefer Horus of the previous Cult. The Eschatology followed this Cult.

Horus in the Eschatology was he who died and was buried and rose again in spirit at his second advent in human form. This time he was imaged in the likeness of his Father, as the beloved and only begotten Son of God, who manifested as the fulfiller of His Word and the doer of His Will. In the Eschatology, Ra became the Great God in Spirit, as the Holy Spirit Father. The two types in this way were deposited and made permanent in Horus, the child of twelve years, and Amsu-Horus, the man of thirty years.

The Christian doctrines arose out of the ashes of this.

The Cult of Atum-Iu lasted about 20,000 years or more.

That of the Sphinx lasted about 10,000 years.

That of Ptah lasted about 9,000 years.

That of Amen lasted about 20,000 years.

That of Osiris lasted about 20,000 years.

The Eschatology about 20,000 years.

The other phases of duality not mentioned above are:

> Tum as the Father, Tem as the son.
>
> Amen-Ra as the Father, Nefer-Atum as the son.
>
> Huhi the eternal God the Father, Iu the son.
>
> Osiris the Father, Horus the son.
>
> Ihuh the eternal Father, Iah the son.
>
> Ieou the Father, Iao the son.
>
> Ihuh the Father, Jesus the son.
>
> Jehovah the Father, Jesus the son.

One must not forget the overlapping that took place in all these Cults.

Many Egyptologists still think and believe that before "prehistoric times" the Egyptians had never promulgated any spiritual conceptions, in our sense of the word. That is a fallacy; they had, but they could only depict it in Sign Language, because they had not the same terminology as we use to-day.

Dr. Wallis Budge states: "Although his [the Egyptian's] ideas were very definite as to the reality of a future existence, I think that he had formulated few details about it, and that he had no idea as to when or how it was to be enjoyed" (*History of the Book of the Dead*, xxxix). The facts found recorded do not bear out Dr. Budge's opinion; evidently Dr. Budge cannot read and understand Sign Language, because, if he could, it would be impossible for him to make such a statement truthfully.

The Book of the Dead or *The Ritual of Resurrection of Life*, as we have it, is principally concerned with the Osirian Cult, which was very late in the history of Egypt, yet the original was all written before the 1st Dynasty, although edited several times after.

There are many passages and chapters (17 and 64, for instance) wherein the Stellar and Lunar Cults are plainly indicated and their beliefs at that remote age.

The later Scribes or old Priests had forgotten the previous wisdom, much of which was passed on orally and all the rest written in Sign Language, but from the earliest times of the Stellar Cult the doctrine of the immortality of the soul and an after-life was most profoundly believed in and worked out, and this was founded in the first place on the faculty of "seership." They had learnt the gnosis of how to communicate with their loved ones who had departed this earthly life, yet they never mourned them, or wept for them, but rejoiced at the time of death, because they knew that they lived again, at least all those who had lived a good life here on this earth. Their "Amenta" or underworld was founded upon the facts that they had ascertained from their departed, and the smallest incidents are left recorded as to what the spiritual body of the departed had to undergo before entering the final Paradise; and only those who had attained that great end were permitted to return and visualize themselves to their friends. These old Wise Men of Egypt did not make any mistake about that—their records prove it; and to one who has learnt and followed this gnosis and "The Periodic Laws," as I have, I have not the slightest hesitation in confirming their beliefs. The materialists of the present day can never obtain that gnosis, because they have never tried to learn, and therefore will for ever remain in dark and dense ignorance on the greatest subject which is most material to their future existence; but it is none the less true, notwithstanding their unbelief, or ignorance, of *The Book of Everlasting Life*—the oldest in the world.

For the proof of my contention, Egypt has

spoken with no uncertain voice, and this is found written in the *Book of the Dead* of Nesi-Khonsu (a priestess of Amen).

For the information of the Brotherhood I will give a translation of part of this remarkable document, as far as concerns our present subject matter:

"This holy God, the lord of all the Gods, Amen-Ra, the lord of the throne of the two lands, the governor of Apt; the holy soul who came into being in the beginning, the great God who liveth by Maat; the first divine matter which gave birth unto subsequent divine matter, the being through whom every (other) God hath existence; the One one who hath made everything which hath come into existence since primæval times when the world was created; the being whose births are hidden, *whose evolutions are manifold, and whose growths are unknown*; the holy Form, beloved, terrible, and mighty in his risings; the lord of wealth, the power, *Khepera, who created every evolution of his existence, except whom, at the beginning, none other existed; who at the dawn in the primæval was Atennu* (*Aten*), the prince of rays and beams of light, who, having made himself (to be seen), caused all men to live."

The above comprises only a few lines translated, but all the Brotherhood can see and read the original, which still exists and has been translated by Maspero and Budge.

The first point of interest in the above is the reference to Apt, the old Earth-Mother, who was divinized in the astro-mythology, and from whom proceeded the seven Elemental Powers—the seven Primary Gods, etc., and who now had been superseded as the Primary One (of *Matriarchal type*) by the *Fatherhood.*

Secondly, we have distinctive evidence of the profound knowledge and belief of evolution, as governed by the Periodic Laws, that the Ancient Brotherhood possessed: "the transformer and creator of new series of cells and forms of matter" being exemplified by the symbolical type of Khepera (Beetle); and—

Thirdly, we have a definite statement that these old ancient Brothers knew and believed in the *only One Great God from the first*, and, moreover, *knew perfectly well the different transformations that had taken place symbolically during the long ages of time, to represent Him, and all the different attributes depicted and portrayed by many signs and symbols* that had grown or had been added to the original as the human race developed in knowledge and wisdom and to a higher type of man.

This remarkable document, the original of which was written in very ancient times (before the Osirian Cult), is well worth the study of Masonic Students, and proves all my contentions as set before the Brotherhood.

CHAPTER IX

MYTHICAL REPRESENTATIONS AND EVOLUTION OF RELIGIOUS IDEAS—THE TEN GREATER MYSTERIES AND RELATIONS OF THE SAME

THE mythical representation did not begin with the human figures at all, but with the phenomena of external nature that were represented by means of animals, birds, reptiles and insects, etc., and various signs and symbols which had demonstrated the possession of superhuman faculties and powers. The origin of various superstitions and customs seemingly insane can be traced to Sign Language. Modern popular superstition, to a large extent, is the ancient symbolism in its childhood. In the most primitive phase mythology was a mode of representing certain Elemental Powers by means of living types that were superhuman, like the natural phenomena, and the foundations of all Ancient Wisdom were laid in the pre-anthropomorphic mode of primitive representation; and this mythical mode of representation went on developing in Egypt, keeping touch with the advancing Arts. Primitive man did not make the mistake about the facts of nature, as we have mistaken the primitive method of expressing them.

Modern ignorance of the mythical mode of representation has led to the ascribing of innumerable false beliefs, not only to primitive man and present-day savages, but also to the most learned, enlightened, and highly-civilized people of antiquity, the Egyptians.

The ignorant representation of the Egyptian Sign Language was begun by the Greeks, who could not read the hieroglyphics or understand their Sign Language. It was repeated by the Romans and has been perpetuated by "Classical Scholars" ever since. But as the interpreter of Egypt that kind of scholastic knowledge is erroneous, and futile as regards the truth of the subject matter.

The Eleusinian and other Mysteries that we find in various countries were originally the Egyptian Mysteries carried out of Egypt by men who had been partially initiated there, and by the various exodes that left the old Motherland for some other countries, and, like their writing, had become perverted and altered by time and circumstances, such as new fauna, which were symbolically the same but different types; innovations crept in when part of the true ritual had been forgotten, as we find amongst the Babylonians and Assyrians, who were first Stellar Cult and were later invaded by the Solar; these converted the Egyptian divinized Elemental Powers, representing all that was beneficent, into all the demons that represented evil. The Greeks are very late as regards human history and evolution, and never understood the gnosis of the Egyptian Wisdom, because they could not read Sign Language or hieroglyphics. Thousands of years even before the Persian Empire existed, the Solar Cult had spread over India and further, to Siam and Java, where they formed a great civilization, as is witnessed by the remains of the old and huge temples still extant at the ruins of Nagor-Wat and Angkorthom. The Solar Cult is at least 100,000 years old and the Stellar over 600,000. But the Solar Cult people, as a great nation, were destroyed in Egypt on account of Socialism and Bureaucracy, and were fast decaying when Greece was only a number of States. The first Minoan civilization of the Mediterranean existed ages before the Greeks (see *The Dawn of Mediterranean Civilization*, by Angelo Mosso), and this civilization only came into being at the time that the Ancient Egyptians were converting their hieroglyphic writing into alphabetical form (Proto-Egyptian of Evans). In studying these ancient peoples one must take into consideration that there was great overlapping. Whilst Central Asia, China, Korea and Japan were still Stellar Cult, in Europe these had been killed off, or the new Solar Cult was imposed upon them and only "remnants" of the Stellar Cult people were left in isolated places. After the destruction of the old Egyptian Empire a dark and degenerate age ensued. Egypt was overrun, her libraries were burnt, her temples destroyed and buried by accumulated filth from Arabs and others, and her learned men slaughtered. The same with the Incas in South America, who were Solar Cult people and formed a huge socialistic-bureaucratic government, and were almost utterly destroyed quickly by the Spaniards. What are these people now?

But members of the old Brotherhood were not all killed; some escaped, and in other countries still continued their rites and Mysteries—although much of the true symbolism was perverted, as the gnosis of the mythical representation had been forgotten, to be found again recently, and to be read once more as the truth, in the language in which it was originally written, *The Ritual of the Resurrection of Egypt in Sign Language.*

Herein can we read and follow throughout the world the old Stellar Cult people and their "Mysteries" — the Chinese, Korean, Japanese and others in many countries of the world, and the old Solar people—the Druids, the Hindus, the Persians, the Incas and the Jews—in all the countries to which they migrated.

The Greeks and Romans, who may be classed as the intermediary nations, only practised a perverted and debased form of the old Egyptian Wisdom.

The Christian doctrine which issued out of the ashes of the old Eschatology, first evolved by the Copts, and the purity of which is spoiled by the recently introduced dogmas, has yet to evolve into a higher and purer Eschatology again.

In the Solar Cult, the Mysteries of Amenta, called the ten Greater Mysteries, were eschatological—Amenta was a symbolic representation of the Earth of eternity, where Taht was the Great Teacher of the secrets, together with the seven masters. The passage through Amenta is a series of initiations for the deceased.

He is inducted into the Mysteries of Rusta (chaps. 1, 7, 9), the Mysteries of the Tuat (chaps. 27, 130), the Mysteries of Akar (chaps. 2, 37, 148). He knows or learns the Mysteries of Nekhen (chaps. 1, 113). The deceased invokes the god who dwells in all the Mysteries (chaps. 1, 14). He learns the Mysteries of the father-god Atum, who becomes his own son (chaps. 15, 46); he is the mysterious of form (chaps. 17, 19) and the mysterious of face (chaps. 9, 133). And the most secret and sacred of the greatest of all Mysteries: its name is the book of the hidden dwelling, that is, the *Ritual of Resurrection* (chap. 162). At the entrance to the Mysterious Valley of the Tuat there is the walled-up doorway, the secret entrance to the Mysteries. It was the first door of twelve divisions of the passage. The rest have open doors and the twelfth a double door. This was typified or symbolically represented by the entrance to the Great Pyramid, where a movable flagstone of a triangular shape revolved over a square stone when the magical word was given. It was called "the Door of Stone." Here is the mystery—how to enter when there is no door and the way is unknown. It is explained to the manes how divine assistance is to be obtained. When the stains of life are effaced, the strength is given for forcing the entrance where there is no door, and in that power the manes penetrate with (or as) the God (chaps. 2, 3, 148).

The entrance to the Great Pyramid (the greatest Masonic Temple ever built) was concealed by means of this movable triangular flagstone that turned on a pivot which none but the initiated could detect. This, when tilted up, revealed a passage, 4 feet in breadth and 3½ feet in height, into the interior of the building. This was a mode of entrance applied to Amenta as the blind doorway, that was represented by the sacred portal and movable stone of later legends. The means of entrance through what appeared to be a blank wall was by knowing the secret of the nicely adjusted stone, and the secret was communicated to the initiate with the password in the Mysteries.

There is no death in the final stage of these doctrines—only decay and change and a periodic renewal; only evolution and transformation in the domain of matter and the transubstantiation into spirit. In the so-called death it is rebirth, not death—exactly the same as in the changes of external nature. If the manes failed at the weighing of his soul, he became annihilated. It would take up too much space to give details of all, but these can be found in the *Ritual* as per *supra*.

It may be of some interest to Brothers of the 18° to know that it was in the "earth of Amenta" that Horus came to restore sight to the blind, and that the *funeral bed should not be recumbent*.

In the D.R. they ought first to arrange the Khen-Kat, "a funeral bed that stands up." The Khen-Kat is the funeral bed on which the dead were laid out in "Amenta," waiting for the coming of Horus, Lord of Resurrection, to wake the sleepers who are in the coffins or lying breathless on the couches. It is the couch of the dead that is set up on end, like the mummy cases with the body inside, which is thus erected on its feet, as a mode of rendering "the Mystery of the Resurrection" or re-erection of the deceased. "Horus causes thee to stand up at the rising. Thou settest forth on thy way." The deceased (or initiate), as the risen mummy, is seen walking off. The drama consists of three acts, with six different characters, in the original Egyptian Mysteries of the passing through Amenta of

Egyptian Wisdom, from the time of the initiate's entering to the coming forth and arrival at Am-Khemen of the Paradise.

There should be two ladders, not one only. The first is the Maget or ladder of Set, typical of the ascent from "*the Land of Darkness.*" The other, the Maget or ladder of Horus, "*reaching to the Land of Light.*"

"He has joined the Lords of Eternity in the Circle of ——" and in the likeness of his own human self, the very figure which he had on earth, but changed and glorified (chap. 178).

The Symbolic Drama is typical of the human spirit passing to its final state.

There are seven Primary Powers in the mythical and astronomical phases; six of these are represented by Zootypes, the seventh is imaged in the likeness of man.

This is represented in the Eschatology, where the highest soul of the seven is the Ka-eidolon, with a human face and figure as the final type of spirit, which was human on earth and is eternal in the heavens, i.e. *the Khu* (spirit).

The Khu is a soul in which the person has attained the status of the "pure spirit," called the "Glorified," symbolically represented in the likeness of a beautiful white bird.

There was still one type or grade higher to attain—the Ka, which is a type of totality and of eternal duration, in which the sevenfold personality is unified at last for permanent or everlasting life. This is where the Hindu and other Mysteries have gone wrong, not knowing the gnosis of the Egyptian Wisdom, the seven Uræus divinities representing the seven souls of life that were anterior to the one enduring soul of, or in, their Eschatology ("My image is eternal," chap. 85), as it would be when the seven souls were amalgamated into one that was imaged by the divine Ka. These seven souls have been conceived as ascending types of personality in human transmigrations on different planes!

In the 18° the Valley of Death is the Egyptian Ar-en-Tet, representing Horus Khent-an-maat, or another name was Horus-Har-Khent-an-arar-f in Sekhem, who was Chief among the manes who were without the means of seeing in the dark. They were blind in the darkness of death in this part of "Amenta."

There is nothing in all poetry, considered as the flower of human reality, more pathetic than the figure of Horus in Sekhem. He has grappled with the Apap of evil and wrestled with Set=the Devil, or Satan, and been overthrown in the passage of absolute darkness. Blind and bleeding from many wounds, he continues to fight with death itself; he conquers, rises from the grave like a warrior with one arm—not that he has lost an arm: he has got only one arm free from the bonds of death, the bandages of the mummy made for the burial. But he lives, he rises again triumphant, *lifting the sign of the Dominator aloft*: and in the next stage of transformation he will be altogether free from the trammels of the mummy, to become pure spirit, in the likeness of the Father, as the express image of His person. He is the *Good Shepherd* who calls to his followers "Hak-er-a" ("Come thou to me"). It was followed by a festival in which there was much eating and drinking.

This is the origin, and original, of the tradition given to Brothers in the 3° of the death of H.A. (who by the by was not killed at all in the building of K.S.T., but lived many years after). Brothers will see how much more sacred and impressive the original is than the "traditional."

In the 17° the original p.w.'s are "Abut-Unti" not "Noddaba." The Egyptian means a form of Apap and typifies non-existence. The A. "Ihuh"=God the Son, who was, as Egyptian, Iu or Hu. Hoshea or Joshua the son of Nun= the Egyptian Shu, and Caleb the son of Jephunneh=Anup-ap-Uat.

The Egyptians represented evil as negation.

Abut-Unti was a form of Apap who was evil, and a type of negation in the natural phenomena, which was opposed to good.

In the Eschatology, Set or Sut represents negation as non-existence.

Evil culminated in annihilation and non-being

for the manes, and the negation of being, of life, of good was the ultimate form of evil.

The hell-fire of Christian Theology, the hell-fire that is unquenchable (Mark ix. 43, 44), is a survival of this representation made in the Egyptian Mysteries.

The manes in Amenta passes through this hell of fire, called the Meskat, in which those who are condemned suffer their annihilation. He says: "I enter in and I come forth from the tank of flame (or lake of fire) on the day when the adversaries are annihilated in Sekhem" (*Ritual*, chap. 1); "I have come from the lake of flame, from the lake of fire and from the field of flame."

This lake of fire that is never quenched was derived from the Solar Force in the mythology, on which the Eschatology was based. The initiate in the Mysteries had to pass through this "lake of fire," which is depicted very graphically in part of the Great Pyramid. We do not now use this "lake of fire," perhaps just as well for the initiates at present, because we have lost the secret connected with this ceremony.

There are, however, some tribes belonging to the Hero Cult Nilotic Negroes who still perform the ceremony in Africa, Asia, America and the Pacific Isles.

They clear a space which they pave with large flat stones; these they make *red-hot* by lighting fires on them, after "a meeting of sacred rites." They walk barefoot all over and about on these whilst still at a red-hot temperature; they do not suffer any distress or scorching in the least—at the same time, an ordinary individual could not approach within a dozen yards on account of the great heat. I am not acquainted with the secrets of the ceremony, but I know that it was a symbolical representation of the "last judgment" in the Greater Mysteries, and those who had failed to make the word of Horus truth against his enemies were doomed to die a second death in the lake of fire.

The first was in the body on the Earth, the second in spirit.

The enemies of justice, law, truth and right were doomed to be destroyed forever in the lake of fire or tank of flame.

They were annihilated once for all into original and separate Corpuscles.

The doctrine occurs in the Pauline Epistles and in Revelation, where the end of all is with destruction in the lake of fire. In the Epistle to the Hebrews the destruction of lost souls is compared with that of vegetable matter being consumed by fire, i.e. the series of Corpuscles which formed this spiritual body, or vegetable matter, *were broken up by fire into the original non-grouped Corpuscles, so that the living spirit was annihilated as a living spirit.* The doctrine, like many others, we see, originated with the Nilotic Negro Hero

Cult people, brought on to the Stellar and Lunar, thence portrayed in their Solar mythology, finally became Eschatological, and thence into the Christian doctrines. It was Egyptian from the first to the last, upon which the haze of ignorance settled down to cause confusion ever since.

The final degree was a very severe test in the Mysteries, and many never attained to that sublime degree.

Entrance to the seven Ārits or mansions of the final test could not be obtained without knowledge and the highest code of morality. The knowledge of the names and attributes of the Doorkeeper (O.G.), Watcher (I.G.), and Herald, who belonged to each, was necessary.

Similarly, the Pylons of the domains of the seven Ārits could not be passed through by the deceased (or initiate) without a declaration *by him* of the names and attributes of each.

Chapter 125 is important to the students of Freemasonry, especially those who take the highest degree.

The deceased or initiate is given or provided with passwords which enable him to enter the Double Maati, or Hall of Judgment, where he is examined—in the Stellar Cult, of the Lesser Mysteries, before seven Judges; in the Greater Mysteries, up to the time of the 18th Dynasty, these had increased to forty-two Judges or "Grand Masters," before whom he had to make his "Negative Confession." From this "Negative Confession" we see that the Egyptian code of morals was the grandest and most comprehensive of those known to have existed amongst any nation, past or present. For the information of all the Brotherhood throughout the world, I give the recitation of our old Brotherhood which each one had to make under penalty of death on the infraction of any or either of them—called the "Negative Confession": "To abhor fraud, theft, deceit, robbery, iniquity of every kind, unchastity or sense of wantonness, manslaughter, murder, incitement to murder, and that he had *wronged* no man in any way." "He honoured his king, and he neither wasted his neighbour's ploughlands nor defiled his running stream. He spake not haughtily, he behaved not insolently, he abused no man, he attacked no man, he swore not at all, he stirred not up strife, he terrified no man, he spake evil of none. He judged not hastily, he defrauded not his neighbour in the market, he shut not his ears to the words of right and truth, he sought not honours, he never gave way to anger except for a proper cause, he sought not to enrich himself at the expense of his neighbours."

After this there was a concluding text uttered by him when he had passed this ordeal of judgment and was beginning a "new life," and the concluding text provides the password which enabled him to go forth from the Double Maati Hall. The Egyptian had no conception of repentance as later taught in the Christian Cult. He based his claim for admission into the Grand Lodge above upon the fact that he had not committed certain sins (*supra*), and that he had feared God and honoured the king, "and gave bread to the hungry, drink to the thirsty, clothes to the naked, and a boat to him that had suffered shipwreck on the Nile." He knew the terrible doom that awaited him from the Judges if he was "not true." He knew their searching inquiries—those could not be deceived; and if his works had been evil he knew that it was not a question of "being sorry." They held the just balance of his works, and upon that judgment was pronounced, and his belief in the efficacy of work was great, and therefore he knew that his sentence would be just—there was "no scruple or diffidence" in the matter—and so was ready to receive his "corn and barley" or his final doom of death.

The seven steps in the 30° are of Lunar Cult origin; a figure of this "mound" may be seen in the vignettes to the *Ritual* as a pyramid with seven steps, called the ladder or staircase of Shu. It is a type of ascent.

The moon fulfilled its four quarters in twenty-eight steps, fourteen up and fourteen down. For this reason, Osiris in the moon was represented by an eye at the top of fourteen steps. The moon in its first quarter took seven steps upwards from the underworld to the summit, which in the annual reckoning was the equinoctial mount. In other words, Shu now made use of a lunar reckoning previously established by the Moon-god Taht, when the Ark of seven cubits was represented by Am-Khemen.

There are two sets of names in the *Ritual* given to the seven steps as Primordial Powers in two of their astronomical characters. The first seven are called (1) An-er-ef the Great, (2) Kat-Kat, (3) the Bull who liveth in his fire, (4) the Red-eyed One in the House of Gauge, (5) Fiery face which turneth backwards, (6) Dark face in its hour, and (7) Şer in the night.

The second seven are (1) Amsta, (2) Hapi, (3) Tuamut'ef, (4) Kabhsenuf, (5) Maa-tef-f, (6) Karbek-ef, and (7) Hai-Khent-an-maa-ti.

The names for the first seven used now are Hebrew importations and have no meaning. The names of the second seven are English substituted ones.

I present the Supreme Council with the true originals, but must abstain from further interpretation of the above on account of secrets connected with the degree.

In the 30° the lost word which some members of the Supreme Couneil travelled to Ireland to obtain, to replace a "substituted one," is still incorrect. The word is "Anhuri," who was "Har-Tesh," the Red God, as the Great Warrior, also as "whose arm was lifted up with the rod or dagger, to keep back, or strike down the evil ones" (the Sebau). "Thou wieldest thy spear

ANHURI OR HAR-TESH.

The Red God as the Great Warrior, also as "whose arm was lifted up with a dagger to keep back or strike down the evil ones" (the Sebau). Shu, the power of the Air, had been divinized as the warrior-god who fought for Horus as leader of the war against the rebel powers of darkness and of drought: 30°. (*Drawn by K. Watkins.*)

to pierce the head of the serpent Nekau" (*Ritual*). I beg to draw the attention of the members of the Supreme Council to this (*supra*).

Horus appears in the various characters of Har-Tema, the revealer of justice; Har-Makheru, the word made Truth, and Har-Tesh, the red god who *orders the block of execution.*

These are phases of Har-Makhu, the God of both horizons, all of which are reproduced in Revelation. Michael, the warrior angel who overthrows "the dragon and his angels," is the Hebrew form of Har-Makhu or Har-Tesh, who is Atum-Hui in the person of his own son. This is Har-Tema, he who makes justice visible in the Cult of Osiris. He is the avenger of the wrongs inflicted on his father by the Apap-dragon and his dark host of the Sebau, or friends of the evil Set, and also by the criminals who, on account of their own deeds, are self-condemned to die the second death upon "the highway of the damned" (*Ritual*, ch. 18).

This "awful tradition of a war in heaven" was made out magnificently in Milton's epic poem, but the original war in heaven was simply elemental, and had no more awfulness or terror in it than a thunderstorm. We can trace this warfare of the elements from the beginning in chaos: the terrors were evoked from the mind of man. A battle was fought each twenty-four hours, and the dragon of darkness is hurled down from the horizon of the east into the pit with all his angels or fiends, called the Sebu or Sami. This great battle, fought in the *Ritual* during the last hours of night, becomes a typical last great battle in a contention that is fought out on the scale of the great year in the Book of Revelation, called "the war of the great day of God the Almighty," when "the kings of the whole world," or kings who ruled in the celestial heptanomis, are to be "gathered together into the place which is called in Hebrew Har-Mageddon" (ch. cvi. 14, 16). This war in heaven, or external nature, was first. Next it was made astronomical. Lastly it was eschatological or theological (see *Ritual*, ch. 30).

Some signs and symbols used by the old Brotherhood and preserved to us during the earlier Christian times, when the remnants of the Brotherhood were persecuted by the priests of Rome, are shown in Mr. Harold Bayley's book *New Light on the Renaissance displayed in Contemporary Emblems.*

By Mr. Harold Bayley's permission, for which I herewith return my sincere thanks, I give some of them.

Here we see the Sacred Axe has been brought on with the addition of the Christian Cross on it; the symbolism of each is the same. Later the Christians took the Axe away and left the Cross only, about the tenth century.

N.B.—The seven Glorious Ones in one portrayal

have been symbolized in the Christian doctrines as the seven Churches.

When Europe was converted to Christianity it was by making use of the same Symbols that were hallowed in the previous Cults, the rooted types being indefinitely more potent than any later sense engrafted on them.

Horus or Jesus as Ichthus, the fish, upon a stone, now in the British Museum. Here we see portrayed the two fishes, one over the head of

Horus and the other under his feet. The latter also repeats the ancient type of the Crocodile on which the divine child was supported in the Cippi of Horus.

In another type of the pictures found in the catacombs the "Good Shepherd" is accompanied by both the lamb and the ram, which are equivalent to the dual types of Horus of the Equinox in Aries. He carries the lamb upon his shoulders, whilst the ram is resting at his feet.

Horus was the lamb on the Western and the ram on the Eastern Horizon, both being united in a figure of the dual power.

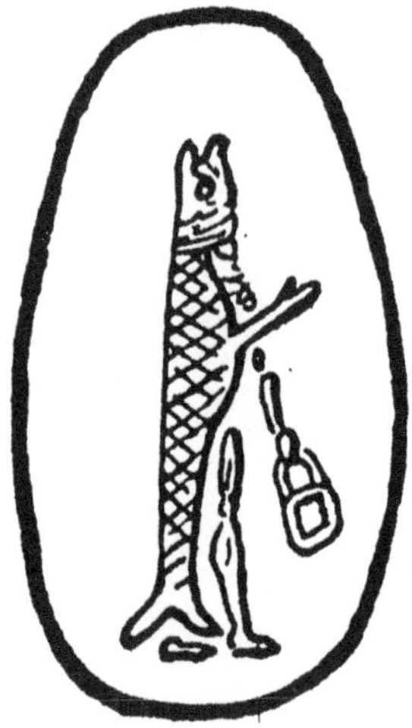

CHALDEAN REPRESENTATION OF THE FISH GOD.

The Fish God of the Assyrians was Horus of the Double Horizon. He is portrayed as a fish. As in the Egyptian, it was a symbolic type as to how he crossed the Horizon from West to East. He swam through the waters of space (see *supra*). (*Drawn by K. Watkins.*)

The mythology remained extant in Egypt, so that the beginning of theology could be known and tested. Egyptian theology was based upon the mythology which preceded it and supplied the mould, and the primitive Mysteries were founded on the facts in nature which are verifiable to-day as from the first. These old Egyptian Mysteries are the originals of all other Mysteries—Gnostic, Kabalistic, Eleusinian, Pythagorean, Zoroastrian, Hindu, Druidic and Jewish, and in fact all, can be traced back to Egypt, and no place on earth can otherwise be found for their origin. Herodotus and other Greek writers are much too late to be of value as regards the ancient past history of the world. Egypt was in a state of decay before the Greeks were born. Herodotus, who was the most reliable Greek historian, tells us, however, of the reluctance of the Egyptians to admit strangers to the holy secrets of their Mysteries. He states that they did, however, admit Eumolpus, King of Eleusis, who on returning to his country instituted the Mysteries of that name which he had learnt from the priests of Egypt, also Orpheus, the Greek poet, the philosopher Thales, and many others.

Herodotus also states (*Euterpe*, L.):

"Egypt has certainly communicated to Greece the names of almost all the Gods."

(LI.) "The Greeks have derived many other customs of religious worship from Egypt."

(LVIII.) "The two oracles of Egyptian Thebes and of Dodona have an entire resemblance to each other. The art of divination as now practised in our temples (Greece) is thus derived from Egypt; at least the Egyptians were the first who introduced the sacred festivals, processions and supplications, and from them the Greeks were instructed. Of this it is to me a sufficient testimony *that these religious ceremonies are in Greece but of modern date, whereas in Egypt they have been in use from the remotest antiquity.*" But what Herodotus knew of the Mysteries he kept religiously concealed.

The description of the "Eleusinian Mysteries" as lately published in the *Freemason* (1919, p. 53), and the article by the critic of the *Occult Review* may be best described as "a criticism of ignorance by ignorance," as far as the real description of the origins and real interpretations are concerned; although this article may interest some Brothers, there can be no doubt that it cannot assist in giving the Brothers who wish to know, any truth of its origin and interpretation; but the above is enough to prove my contention. These men not understanding the true gnosis or Sign Language, the translations became debased and none of the truth remained. The Druids, who were the priests of the old Solar Cult in Europe and these Isles, carried away from the first a *true interpretation*, although, as time went on, much of the original was forgotten by their descendants, communications having been cut off from the original home, which was now destroyed, and innovations became substitutes for the originals. These continued their old ceremonial rites until the order of Canute, and practised them long after in secret places, forming secret "Lodges." Later, many of the secret and sacred rites found their way to Scotland and other parts of Britain from the Continent and Asia in a perverted form, finally forming the so-called Speculative Lodge here.

Ireland appears to have retained a truer form of the original than any other country, possibly because we know that direct communication was maintained from Egypt to Ireland by the Her-Seshsta to comparatively late periods, and Ireland, being isolated, did not have so much communication with the rest of the priests of Europe, who exercised a form perverted from the original. In America and Asia both the Stellar and Solar Cult remained until the advent of the Christian Roman Religion, brought over by the Spaniards.

As showing how some of the Christian was taken from the Egyptian, I reproduce these five bulls' heads, with other symbols. They are very interesting and important as showing how the old Egyptian Sign Language was brought on and converted into the Christian symbolism.

The original bull's head alone was purely Egyptian, and was one of the ideographic symbols for Horus of the Double Horizon, or Double Equinox,

FIG. 1.

The head of a Bull with the symbol of Amsu or the Risen Christ of the Egyptians. One of the earliest symbols for Horus of the Primary Solar Cult, when Hathor represented the Mother as a Cow on one Horizon and Horus, her child, as a young Bull on the other.

FIG. 3.

This shows the Bull's head (Horus of the Double Horizon symbol) with the *Christian Cross only* depicted above, the symbol for Amsu having been left out entirely. The next phase was that they did away with the head of the Bull and left the Cross only. Probably about the fifteenth or sixteenth century.

FIG. 2.

This shows how the Christians brought on and converted the old symbolism into the present. Here is depicted the head of a Bull with the Christian Cross on the head, and above this the old symbol for Amsu. Probably about the eighth or tenth century.

before the human type had been depicted, when it was the Cult of Hathor and Horus. Horus was represented as the Calf on one Horizon and the Bull on the other. In the primary Solar mythos, child Horus was symbolized as the little autumn sun, conceived on the Western Mount as the Calf or Child. Adultship was attained upon the Eastern Horizon with what is termed the double force. In these two characters he was the Double Horus

FIG. 4.

Figs. 4 and 5 "Bull's heads" represent the earliest formation of Set and Horus brought on from the Lunar Cult. Each is typified by its ideographic sign or symbol. No. 4 is Horus with the fleur-de-lys or white lily, which is brought on in the 18°, and represented by the "Lily of the Valley."

FIG. 5.

Represents Set, and is typified by the ideographic hieroglyphic for hide or animal, and in this case would represent the giraffe, or Okepi, or Set animal.

or the Double Harmachis—the Solar god on both Horizons, and fulfilled annually in the Double Equinox. The power of evolution was portrayed in Kheper, the transformer, as Kheper showed the old beetle changing into the young, the tadpole transforming into the frog, the human embryo developing *in utero*, the enduring spirit emanating from the mortal mummy. Kheper was a form of Har-Makhu, as we learn from the Sphinx.

In Fig. 1 we observe the symbol of Horus (the little Pygmy sacred sign) as Atum-Iu or the Risen Amsu-Atum Iu, this being a symbol also for Horus of the Double Horizon.

In Fig. 2 we have the bull's head with the Christian Cross above and between the two horns (two horns being a symbol of Solar ascent), and above the cross again we have the Pygmy sacred sign, which is now the ideographic symbol for Amsu or Atum-Iu, or "the Risen Christ" both of the Egyptians and Christians.

In Fig. 3 we have the bull's head, but the Christians have done away with the Egyptian ideograph and substituted the Christian Cross in its place. At the same time the interpretation of the symbols is all one and the same, as I have demonstrated and proved in Fig. 71, p. 193, in *Arcana of Freemasonry*, showing that the Shamash of the Chaldeans, Babylonians and Assyrians was the Egyptian Atum-Iu or Horus of the Double Horizon. The symbolicy is identical in all cases. Figs. 4 and 5 show the primary and originals.

I also reproduce two ladders which have been brought on in the early Christian symbolism from the Egyptian originals. One, the Ladder of Shu, with his symbol depicted above. The other the Ladder of Horus, with his house or Paradise portrayed above; but the early Christians have only shown three steps in each case instead of seven, and in their portrayal of Paradise, or the

House of Horus, they have depicted a six-pointed star instead of the Egyptian five.

The five-pointed star was a symbol of the House of Horus or Paradise. The original six-pointed star of the Egyptians represented the six "Glorious Ones" or the six Primary Powers uranographically represented by the constellation of Ursa Minor or Little Bear—the stars that never set as seen from Old Egypt, with Horus as the seventh, and the portrayal originated during the

SHU.

HORUS.

Stellar Cult. The Christians have put one too many points to the star and left out the central . (dot), which represented Horus as the seventh and the greatest one. A later representation was the seven stars as seven Powers, and Horus was added as the eighth by the . in the centre.

Horus was the teacher of the Lesser Mysteries in his first advent—that is, the Stellar Cult—and teacher of the Greater Mysteries in his second—that is, the Solar Cult.

I also reproduce three Symbols of Ṣet or Sut as brought on by the early Christians. In one attitude we see him as fighting; this was later

brought on as the Unicorn opposite the figure of the Lion (the latter being one of the symbols for Horus).

We see here another example of how the old symbolism was first brought on into the Christian doctrines and then discarded.

This is a "compound symbolism" of different periods of time. The two doves represent Hathor and her child as Horus. Hathor is on, or within, her Tree, which is supported in the Sektet boat; Horus is at the prow of the boat, which is supported on the back of the Crocodile which swam the waters of space to Paradise. Here he lands the manes and presents to his Father.

Probably about the fifth or sixth century.

I am indebted to a Brother in Australia for sending this interesting picture.

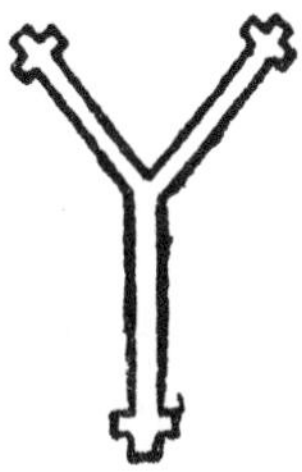

This is another symbol thus brought on from the Stellar Cult. It was the original Stellar Cult Swastika (see *Arcana of Freemasonry*, Fig. 116,

p. 288, for the original and full explanation). It is the figure of the tripartite division of the Ecliptic, represented symbolically by Horus, God of the North, Set, God of the South, and Shu, God of the Equinox—the Primary Trinity—and the triangle in the centre represents Horus as the One Great God. The original, as perceived, has been altered with the Christian symbolism by substituting the three crosses in place of the originals and leaving out the central triangle (G).

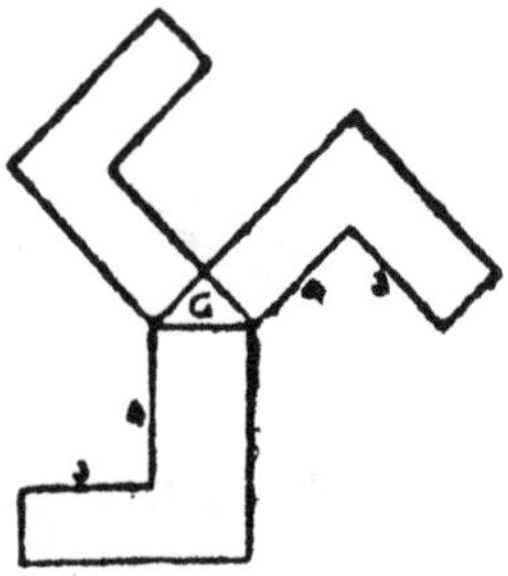

Swastika with Three Arms. Stellar Cult.

This is used by the York Division only.

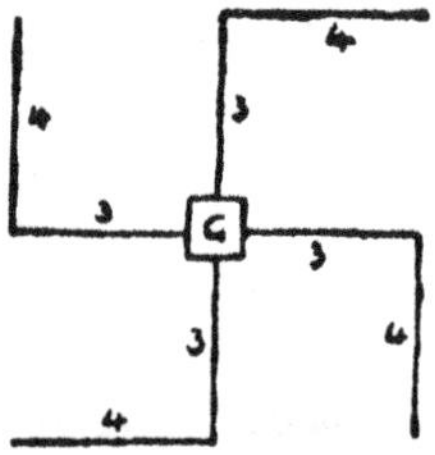

Swastika with Four Arms. Solar Cult.

This is used by all eight Divisions, and represents the four divisions of Heaven.

Mr. Harold Bayley has done a great service in producing some of these figures, although I cannot always agree with his decipherment. There are many more in his book, all of which are of Egyptian origin, but what I have shown *supra* is sufficient for my contention here. Brothers can find no written records—except in ancient writings and

Sign Language—" of the first meeting of Lodges," here in the British Isles or elsewhere, because there were no written records of present-day terminology and writing.

The old first Christian monks in Europe would, and did, take great care that all writings, or traces of writings, of the old Cults were destroyed, or at least all that they could not make use of and carry on in that new Cult: moreover, the old Christian monks were about the only men who could write at the time. It was a dark and ignorant age; for hundreds of years the people depended upon what the priests told them, and these were not much better informed as to the truth than the poor ignorant classes. But for all Brothers who take an interest in the origin and real meaning of the rites and ceremonies of our Order, there in the *Ritual* of Egypt, written in Sign Language, lies the true origin of all the Mysteries in the world, and in the study of the origin and evolution of the human race can be traced the reasons for the foundation of the same.

Not "trailing clouds of glory" have we come from any state of perfection as fallen angels in disguise, with the trump of attainment all behind us, but as animals, emerging from the animals, wearing the skins of animals, uttering the cries of animals, whilst developing our own; and thus the nascent race has travelled along the course of human evolution with the germ of immortal possibilities in it, darkly struggling for the light, and a growing sense of the road being up-hill, therefore difficult, and not to be made easy like the downward way to nothingness and everlasting death.

CHAPTER X

UNIVERSAL BROTHERHOOD OF FREEMASONRY THE ONLY EFFECTIVE MEANS FOR PERMANENT PEACE THROUGHOUT THE WORLD

IF the ostensible ends of the Peace Society are ever attained, they will be accomplished by the Universal Brotherhood of Freemasonry combined, as this is the only effective means for *permanent Peace* throughout the world.

The difficulty is one that can be overcome only by the progressive evolution to a higher type of Homo, which is governed by the Periodic Laws of the Corpuscles. Thus man, depending on his evolution, will be advanced or retarded by the struggles between individuals and States obeying, or not, the fundamental Laws of Nature. These Periodic Laws of T.G.A.O.T.U. are true and immutable, and although we have dark and degenerate ages, decay and obliteration of erring nations in the world's history, yet we find that evolution of the human race is progressive.

Man ought to be ever striving to help the Divine evolution by becoming to the best of his ability well instructed and informed. True education in every sense of the word, with congenial and healthy surroundings and good food, would tend to produce a larger number of series of corpuscles with less inclination to part with one or more corpuscles at the terminal end of the normal series, thus producing a better balanced brain and mind. Civilizations made up of individuals who refuse to travel the road that leads to complete development, and by selfishness and greed reach seeming prosperity, only waste away and die without having grasped the duty of every race, namely, to receive and pass on to posterity the message of truth—these seek to dominate and control the life and conscience of the individual and subject him to tyranny and bondage.

Now we come to the question, "Is Freemasonry a Failure?" To one who has made a deep study for forty years, and can read and understand the Ancient Glyphs, which give a history of the past rise and fall of all great nations, and the causes for the same, as well as the progressive evolution of the human race, the answer is, at this date: It has not been, and is not now, a failure; but at the present time English Freemasonry is in the very gravest sense at a critical period, with the balance of the scales at equipoise. This statement is true, because, when studying the progressive evolution of the human race, it is not difficult to understand why the present humans here in England, in this supposed enlightened period, should have acted and set themselves against the Periodic Laws of the Universe, which are true and immutable—that have been, are, and will for all eternity be in active operation. Hitherto in this country (England), the Government at least have neglected and despised science; they have not understood that it is simply the whole of human experience ordered and classified. A State that tries to govern its affairs without science is blind; every step it takes is a step in unexplored ground, and it only learns by bitter experience the folly and disaster that follow such a course. If a nation permits a Socialistic, Bureaucratic Government to be set up at its head at this period of the evolution of the human race, there can be only one end; the principle of this kind of government is to augment official power, official members, with undue influence or authority—officials who govern by a rigid and arbitrary routine, causing delay, muddle, extravagance, red tape, corruption and scandalous waste. The people are not given a chance of developing on true human lines—that is to say, the laws of natural evolution of the development of the human race have been stultified; the system of education is to make the individual a unit in the machine of State, and the individual is merely an accessory part, all his best instincts are stifled, only blind obedience and servility being taught.

Freemasonry, on the contrary, teaches and inculcates those principles which, if followed, will build character, increase intelligence, foster self-reliance, promote independent thinking, abolish fear, annihilate superstition, spread love and goodwill everywhere; it possesses the highest and truest ethics which the world has ever seen. One of these has been, and is, the unfaltering, courageous and consistent championing of individual life, individual liberty, and individual happiness against the other force of Bureaucracy, which, with equal persistency, is seeking to dominate and control the life, intelligence and conscience of the individual, and subject him to individual bondage and servitude. Unfortunately, many Freemasons have been, and are, assisting in this latter disastrous course, and, if pursued, Freemasonry will become a total failure. The question is whether our Brotherhood has learnt the bitter lesson that has already been taught in the past for the survival and continuation to a higher type of evolution of our race, and, therefore, the continuation of Freemasonry in this country to a higher standard; and for it not to be a failure, Brethren must learn to use, and not work against, those Laws which T.G.A.O.T.U. has given as a guide for our future welfare—the Periodic Laws of the Universe. If we still persist in supporting Socialistic Bureaucracy, we shall become a failure and go under. The penalty of sin is death, and the sin in this case is not only neglect, but actual active operation against the laws of evolution and the universe, which will, and must, lead to disaster and destruction of the British Empire, and, therefore, to Freemasonry in this country. However much some Brethren may differ from me in this opinion, which is founded upon the knowledge of the Periodic Laws of the Universe and the past history of the fall of all great nations, it is a fact that Bureaucratic Governments, through want of knowledge and ignoring scientific truths, are producing such a state that there can be only one possible end to any country, and to Freemasonry in that country, where such fettered Governments are adopted. Freemasonry will not live in the future to perform its allotted task by simply being a charitable club and good-fellowship.

Freemasonry is something more than this. Thousands of years ago T.G.A.O.T.U. gave the old Wise Men of Egypt the written laws for life everlasting, as well as a "doctrine of final things." These the human race has never been permitted to lose, and the foundation of our Brotherhood was built on these solid rocks. Although we have travelled far and long since our "originals" were in existence, and we therefore have many innovations in our Rituals on account of compilers of latter days not understanding the originals, yet the "substance" has never been lost. In these laws not only have we the spiritual side, but our duties regarding our country and fellow-men are laid down as a guide for our future actions. We have the experience, and therefore knowledge, given to us for the causes of the fall of all great nations in the past, and with their fall we know how the learned Brethren of each country were murdered, or driven forth to other countries, there to rise again and form great nations. As long as a nation has continued to follow the Divine and immutable Laws of the Universe, T.G.A.O.T.U. has prospered and assisted that nation to advance to a higher state of evolution. *Wars will never cease until the whole of the human race has attained that higher evolution;* if the lower type of man will not progress in the way the Divine Creator has appointed, he will be destroyed, and if one nation which has risen to the highest state of evolution then ignores and acts against these laws, it is acting against T.G.A.O.T.U., and the result will always be the same—destruction and disintegration, and another nation will rise and take its place. Freemasonry, therefore, which has risen to a higher and better state of evolution in this country, is now in the balance. But let no Brother think for one moment that Freemasonry will be destroyed universally. That will never be. If we fail here to perform our allotted task, Freemasonry will progress in another nation and be carried to a higher point in evolution. If the Brother who feels he needs further direction in order to obtain a stronger faith and a larger hope will remember the origin, study the laws, carry out these, together with the tenets taught in his Lodge, in his daily life, he need have no fear for the future, but he should make himself acquainted with all the so-called Degrees in Freemasonry, because in the Craft and R.A. Lodges he has only part of the Ritual and his duties unfolded to him; whereas in all the Degrees the duty of man to himself and the world, as well as to all his Brethren, is set forth, and although some of these are apparently of modern origin, such is not really the case: they are but innovations made to supply the part of the "Ritual of the Resurrection of Life" which has not been known to the modern compilers. It is for the Brotherhood of Freemasons to recognize the Laws of the Universe and follow them as T.G.A.O.T.U. has ordained, if they do not wish to be scattered over the face of the earth and water again. If the peace of the world and universal brotherhood is to be attained, it will be done through and by Freemasons, and not by *Socialism and Bureaucracy, for these latter are responsible for the destruction of every great nation that has perished, without any exception*, as the past history of the world proves, and are directly opposed to the Periodic Laws. If England is to be saved from following the fate of Russia, and Freemasonry is to flourish and not be a failure, the Brethren must light their lamps, otherwise they will be left to perish and represent the Foolish Virgins. They have only to remember the past history of Old Egypt, their Motherland, whose temples became hopelessly abandoned and hidden beneath the accumulated filth of generations of Arabs. Their Great Library was burnt to ashes, their Wise Men were slaughtered, or driven forth to find a home in another land, and the latest example, where history has repeated itself, is quite recent. The Socialists and uneducated classes in Russia have revolted against the educated classes: Socialism in its worst form has been preached and let loose, with the result—the destruction of the very thin layer of educated people that it had taken Russia centuries to collect. Where they murder their officers and generals of experience and put common soldiers in command, and tramp soldiers and sailors to administer the revolutionary courts, murder their physicians and surgeons and establish common house-porters in their places, all law and order must disappear, to be replaced by anarchy, civil war, starvation, and breaking up of a mighty empire, and the progress of the evolution of this part of the human race will have to begin again, dating back a thousand years. They will have to begin from the bottom of the ladder of civilization. If Freemasonry is not to be a failure, it must take such action that a similar fate shall not befall this country, although we appear to be running headlong in that direction; these are not idle words, but sure deductions drawn from immutable laws. If Freemasonry is not to be a failure, the Brethren must follow and practise those teachings outside the Lodge that they are taught inside. It will not be sufficient to subscribe to the Institutions and be a "good fellow." Freemasonry is more than that. It is the old true religion of the world, without dogmas or sects, and to preserve Freemasonry from failure it must be acted on and taught as such in our lives. If we fail to obey the Laws of T.G.A.O.T.U., we must not complain or be surprised if He destroys us. It would be we have failed, and not Freemasonry or the "Ritual of Resurrection and the Life to Come." That still stands good where it did 300,000 years ago and more.

If Masonry needed to be justified for imposing political as well as moral duties on its initiates, it would be enough to point to the sad history of the world. It would not even need that she should turn back the pages of history to the chapters written by Tacitus; that she should recite the incredible horrors of despotism under Caligula and Domitian, Caracalla and Commodus, Vitellius and Maximin. She need only point to the centuries of calamity through which the French nation passed: to the long oppression of the Feudal Ages, of the selfish Bourbon Kings: to those times when the peasants were robbed and slaughtered by their own lords and princes like sheep: when the lord claimed the first-fruits of the marriage-bed: when the captured city was given to merciless rape and massacre: when the State prisons groaned with innocent victims, and the Church blessed the banners of pitiless murderers and sang *Te Deums* for the crowning mercy of the Eve of St. Bartholomew, and when the Pope's Nuncio and the Cardinal de la Roche-Ayman, devoutly kneeling one on each side of Madame du Barry, their King's abandoned prostitute, put the slippers on her naked feet as she rose from the adulterous bed. Then, indeed, the people were beasts of burden. Why has France risen again in all her glory? Because France has seen that man is supreme over institutions, and not they over him. Man has natural empire over all institutions. They are for him, *according to his developments:* not he for them. Man owed it to himself to be free. He owed it to his country to seek to give her freedom and to maintain her in that possession. It made tyranny and usurpation the enemies of the human race. It created a general outlawry of despots and despotisms, temporal and spiritual. The sphere of duty was intensely large. Patriotism had henceforth a new and wider meaning. Free government, free thought, free conscience, free speech—all these came to be inalienable rights, which those who had parted with them, or been robbed of them, or whose ancestors had lost them, had the right to retake. Civil and religious freedom must go hand in hand. Free government grows slowly, like the individual human faculties. Liberty is not only the common birthright, but it is lost as well by non-user as by mis-user. It depends far more on the universal effort than any other human property. France has to thank Masons for the freedom she possesses now, and France will rise to a higher, freer, and happier state, the individuality and independence of her people will assert themselves, and Freemasonry will flourish in France more than it ever did before in all her history. In her Lodges she has recognized T.G.A.O.T.U., but she has obliterated for ever the Church dogmas. And what of Italy? The trite tale is the same. Rome, more intolerant of heresy than of vice and crime, came to fear the Templar Order. It has always deemed philosophical truth a dangerous heresy, and has never been at a loss for a false accusation to try to crush free thought. One has only to mention all the persecutions that the Brotherhood have suffered from Rome. But they have at last risen to be a free and independent people, with Masonry as the foundation of their faith. One has only to consider the teachings of Masonry. In the whole teachings there is not a single false principle of ethics, there are no fetters to break. Science and Masonry *are necessary to checkmate the secret and well-understood effort now being made to gain control of, and to subvert the original purpose of, our dearly-won freedom.* From the dawn of civilization to the present moment two active and opposing forces have been engaged in deadly conflict over the destinies of human intelligence. One of these—Freemasonry—has been the unfaltering, courageous, and constant champion of individual life, individual liberty and individual happiness. The other has, with equal consistency and persistency sought to dominate and control the life, intelligence and conscience of the individual, and subject him to individual bondage and servitude. The one has dignified and emphasized the individual intelligence and appreciated its value, both to itself and to society. The other has persistently ignored the great fundamental fact in Nature that the individual in his own right, as such, is vested with certain indefeasible attributes and certain inalienable rights, privileges and benefits which must be respected. The profound philosophy and science locked up in the symbolism of Freemasonry has come down to us from the Eschatology of Ancient Egypt. It was the common bond and the religion of the human race all over the world 300,000 years ago. Through the dark ages of the last 5,000 years its temples had been thrown down, its blazing star had been eclipsed, and the old Brothers had been put to fire and sword; but Freemasonry has risen again, its Brothers have fought for the freedom of the world, and that great stronghold of Freemasonry, the United States of America, joined the Allies to fight for right, justice, morality, truth, and freedom for humanity from tyranny and oppression.

The Masonic force to-day finds its nucleus for a universal undogmatic and unfettered manifestation in our world-wide Institution. Against this there is another force, its field of operation being in an organized body that seeks to maintain itself without regard to the largest measure of individual liberty and enlightenment. Upon one side stands an Institution that has "from time immemorial and through a succession of ages" given light to all its votaries. Upon the other side are entrenched Socialism and Bureaucracy, an organization that champions ignorance, superstition and fear, and that dominates and controls the reason and conscience of its communicants.

How many of the Brotherhood throughout the world are working, truly trying to carry out the duty that is morally imposed upon them as Freemasons, to attain this higher evolution of the Brotherhood and the human race? I say unto every Brother, of every clime and of whatever creed, that this is a duty which devolves upon him by the Laws and Tenets of our Order.

Let all those who doubt me attend the full Ceremony and Working of the Ritual of the 4° —"The Secret Master"—and those other higher Degrees which unfortunately in many places are "confirmed" on the Brother and not worked *in extenso.*

I believe that this is the reason and cause why many Brothers do not know or comprehend that this duty is taught and imposed upon them as Freemasons.

But let that be no excuse for a Brother; he should make himself acquainted with the whole Ritual of Freemasonry and the meaning of the same. If this were done, it would be a convincing proof of that which I write.

The unfortunate attitude observed by the governing bodies of Grand Lodges renders a closer union of a universal Brotherhood for the government of the world, and obviously universal peace, still remote. But, Brethren, this will come, because there are many Freemasons who are working out the destiny and will of T.G.A.O.T.U. to this end. Because we have many Brothers at the head of our grand Institution who are ignorant of the origin and meaning of our Ritual, even unacquainted with many parts of the whole Ritual of Freemasonry and the working of the same, that is no reason why we should despair or be downhearted.

Consider the great advance that has been made within the last hundred years and the enormous increase to the ranks of the fraternity; amongst them, within the last fifty years, there are many who wish and want to know, who feel and see that there is more in Freemasonry than a just common Brotherhood and Charity, who know that our doctrines have originated and been handed down pure and unsullied from the Eschatology of the Ancient Egyptians, and that none of the many creeds now in existence—the offshoots from the original—can be compared with the purity and high moral standard, pointing our duty to God and man and as a guide to our action, of the Ritual of our Brotherhood. As our strength becomes greater, as our experience becomes more extensive, you can no longer confine the Brotherhood within swaddling bands, or lull them in the cradle, or amuse them with metaphysical terminology, or try to terrify them with some bugbear of infancy. Men of the twentieth century cannot govern as did men of the eighteenth and nineteenth centuries. Since then so much experience has been gained, and experience is true knowledge.

Will those Brothers who govern the Craft seize this opportunity (in these I include all the Grand Lodges of our Empire and those of all our Allies)? And I say such an opportunity for unity and the discussion of such world-wide problems which have now arisen may never occur again. Alas! I am afraid we shall look in vain to those who govern the Craft and to whom we are told to look for guidance and direction; we shall have to wait for more enlightened men—men who do not set their faces against the very laws they are supposed to support and uphold. Brothers, these are strong words, but it is the truth we want—truth, and truth always. Let Brothers judge my words after attending the full working of the 4°. That part of the Ritual alone is proof of what I have written. But Brothers are beginning to take more rational and comprehensive views of our Ritual. We are not, we cannot in the nature of evolution of things be, what our fathers were: we are no more like the men of one hundred years ago; there is a change, and at present a very bloody change, taking place. This change does not end in nothing; therefore see you guide that movement which you cannot stop. Fling wide the gates to that force which else will enter through the breach. Then will it still be, as it has been hitherto, the peculiar glory of our Constitution to add to our titles of glory the noblest and purest ethics of the attainment of universal peace. Men are apt to deride what they do not understand, and the ignorant, being aware of the weakness of their minds, condemn that which they ought most to venerate.

And what is there to prevent the combination of a Universal Brotherhood who will say, "There shall be no war now, or at any future time"? Nothing that could not be easily overcome. There should be, in the first place, *One Grand Lodge* for every country. However many Provincial or State Grand Lodges there may be, it would not matter provided they were all under the jurisdiction of the One Grand Lodge of that country.

Secondly, no Lodge shall admit any Brother who does not profess to believe in T.G.A.O.T.U., and no Lodge shall be included in the Universal Brotherhood which does not acknowledge T.G.A.O.T.U. To do so would at once shatter the corner stone of the very foundation upon which the Brotherhood has been founded, and to which it owes its existence—not only now, but from its very inception 300,000 years ago. The very foundation of Masonry is the belief in T.G.A.O.T.U. and an after-life, which we know does exist; if, therefore, materialists were admitted, the whole structure on which it has been built becomes a foundation of sand only. We at once do away with the Great Creator of All, and He would do away with us. It has been only because we have believed in Him and kept to His Divine Law that we have prospered and become again a Great Brotherhood.

Therefore, if each country formed One Grand Lodge, holding jurisdiction and alliance over their Provincial or States Grand and other Lodges, it would not be difficult to arrange for all "Grand Masters," with a certain number of G.O., to meet at given intervals and decide the best method of procedure.

I think if the U.S. of America would follow what I have suggested (*supra*) and form One Grand

Lodge for the U.S., representing all other States' Grand and other Lodges *at once*, it would be a great inducement for other countries to do the same, and one of the principal difficulties would disappear. It would be founded then as on the principles of the G.L. of England. If this union of the Brotherhood were accomplished, and I see no reason why it could not be quietly accomplished, it would be worth all the navies and armies in the world, and universal peace could be insisted on *for all time.*

I have suggested this in many former articles in various papers and in my books, and it now rests with the Brotherhood throughout the world to achieve this great end and prevent such suffering and horrors as are still being enacted and have been for the last four years.

We see now the repetition of the destruction of Great Nations which have gone against the Divine Periodic Laws, and ours will follow rapidly in their wake if this is not altered. Russia will take a thousand years to recover her state of evolution. What a lesson to those who will learn and take heed of the Laws of Evolution! Anarchy, murder, starvation, and all the horrors too numerous to write, and all caused by Socialism and Bureaucracy, and so the poor humanity of Russia will return to a dark and degenerate age, to begin again to climb the ladder of light, which will take her a thousand years before she reaches the top.

Another difficulty may arise *pro tem.* from the cause of lack of knowledge to understand what true Freemasonry is, and all the duties that are incumbent upon the members of the Brotherhood.

The *majority* of Freemasons know nothing really of what Freemasonry represents. To them it is a charitable Brotherhood, a kind of semi-religious social club. There are others, however, who are striving to learn and to know; their conscience tells them that there is something more in this great, wonderful Brotherhood than charity and social club, which holds them together in one firm bond. Let them continue their studies. Light will be given them. But nothing comes to him who does not work and strive to gain knowledge. The gaining of the true conception of what Freemasonry was and is will strengthen their belief in the Divine Creator, because they will begin to understand His Laws, and, therefore, His wishes; it will further induce them to carry in their daily lives, outside our Temples, and act with regard to their other fellow-creatures, all those grand principles and tenets that are taught inside the Temples. It will teach them that Socialism, Bureaucracy and *Anarchy* are all tyranny, and must be put down if they wish to attain a higher state of evolution; because all these phases of Socialism are diametrically opposed to the Periodic Laws, which are the Laws of the

Divine Creator—and you cannot serve two masters; you must be true to yourself, to your God, and to man, or you will fail, and ultimately be destroyed morally and spiritually, although probably you may gain much gold; but what will that serve you eventually? You are born naked into the world, your material life is very short, only a few years at most, and then what for eternity? I tell you all, my Brothers, because after forty years of hard study I have been permitted to know and learn these Divine Truths, both as regards this material world and also the Divine Laws of the Spiritual and Everlasting State, and I therefore write for you the TRUTH.

If the League of Nations be formed, *that will not prevent the repetition* of the "Great Horror" in fifty or one hundred years hence, although it would be an excellent work and might have the desired effect for many years. But no guarantee as such "an international combination" could last one hundred years. The Treaty, and even the action, of the League would be treated as "a scrap of paper" or be broken, because the necessary cohesion of all nations could not exist so long on that alone. Greed and other interests would overcome the weakest.

Whereas with the Brotherhood it will be for ever growing in strength and insuperable: there are no opposing principles or interests; all the ties would be strengthened and become firmer.

There could be no divergent opinions or interests in any way or any form. Our Laws have been laid down for us from the first, and these are God's Laws. There would always be the one great sacred tie for the life here and hereafter, for the good of all the Universal Brotherhood; this would be an imperishable bond, with every link forged of the sacred "Ba metal," unbreakable and untouchable as long as this world lasts.

And how has Freemasonry grown within the last two hundred years? One has to look back only to the 24th of June 1717, when there met in the City of London an assembly of Freemasons, representing the membership of four Lodges, under the chairmanship of the oldest Freemason then present. The assembly organized itself into a Grand Lodge.

Within ten years there was formed a Grand Lodge in Ireland, and within twenty one was formed in Scotland.

All regular Masonic Lodges in the world have derived their authority directly or indirectly from one or other of these first three Grand Lodges. Freemasons now number over two millions throughout the world and are growing in number every year. What was Freemasonry, then, prior to this London Conference in 1717?

It might be compared to little rivers all issuing from an underground "Lake of Knowledge," the source of these little rivers being unknown, except to a few, it being hidden away amongst impenetrable forests and mountains.

But the source, or "Lake of the Waters of Knowledge and of Truth," was there nevertheless; that hitherto few had been able to explore these regions and find the Fount was because no one could read the Sign Posts of the Path.

Well, Brothers, I have given you the position in latitude and longitude, and pictured before your eyes "The Fount of all our Mysteries." Therefore, let no one imagine 1717 marks the origin of Freemasonry. There are authentic manuscript copies of old constitutions and charges which prove incontestably the existence of working Lodges as early as the thirteenth century in this country.

The so-called Regius Manuscript of the old charges in the British Museum is definitely known to date from the fourteenth century. Both this manuscript and the next oldest—the Cooke Manuscript, also in the British Museum, which palæographers assign to the early years of the fifteenth century—speak of Freemasonry as having originated in Egypt and having been introduced into England in the reign of King Athelstane, who reigned in the tenth century; and, as I have stated and proved, both the Stellar and Solar Cult were established here thousands of years before that, the former having the Lesser Mysteries and the latter (the Druids) practising the Greater Mysteries.

Certainly, about two hundred years ago these rivers of "Masonic influence" rushed forth from their concealed sources into the light of day, and it is only by tracing these small rivers back along their "meandering way" mile by mile that I have been able to give you the position and origin of that "Great Lake of Knowledge" from which they issued, with absolute certainty.

Now all should unite in one great river and amalgamate in the "Pool of Universal Brotherhood" to erect amidst the waters that "Great Lighthouse" which has been so long required to brighten the dark and turbulent sea of humanity, so that they may travel in their "Barque of Life" for ever in Peace and safety. Brothers, do not be deceived into thinking that cultivating a regular attendance at rehearsals, memorizing the Ritual, paying visits and feeling that by the degree of culture to be obtained through painstaking adherence to these practices you may hope not only to become familiar with the forms and routine of the Lodge, but also to be enabled with confidence to make a speech—is Freemasonry; unfortunately, this, in brief, is the limit to be obtained according to the views of many Brothers, and also this is in accordance with the modern tendency to regard Freemasonry from an external standpoint, with the result that a false value is placed on perfection of ceremonial and individual adeptness. Viewed in this light, our Brotherhood can hardly be said to differ from a charitable and social debating club, or any other gathering where harmony and self-improvement are cultivated.

This is not Freemasonry, and the little rivers that follow this course will flow in the desert sand and be lost there.

Unfortunately, "the powers that be" up to the present have not helped much to assist this "unity of streams."

I have given you the origins, evolutions and meanings of the Brotherhood of Freemasonry, and I trust I have inculcated in your brains the great Divine principles you have inherited from your old Ancestors—a priceless gift; and it rests with you—every individual Brother—to assist and carry out the great truths and principles with which you are so well acquainted, and to assist in forming that "one great Universal Brotherhood again," which once existed thousands of years ago, for procuring the Peace of the World, and as His servants and instruments establishing a higher evolution of Humanity, as T.G.A.O.T.U. has decreed.

Let us save the world from a repetition of the horrors that have been enacted in this last Great War and the sufferings of poor helpless humanity that have been caused as the result of this war. Let us unite and prevent such anarchy and human destruction as is now being enacted in Russia and other countries, throwing these countries and the poor humans back in evolution, and consigning them to a dark and degenerate age again for a thousand years, and is now threatening this country in an acute form. But do not mistake "the means or the way" to accomplish this. There is only one way, i.e. following the Periodic Laws of the Universe, which are God's immutable Laws since the Creation. There is only one means, "A United and Universal Brotherhood throughout the World."

But, mark well, that Universal Brotherhood cannot include members of the Craft who do not believe in T.G.A.O.T.U.

It cannot include all those members of the Craft who support those who practise tyranny and oppression, and all those who seek to dominate and control the life, intelligence and conscience of the individual and subject him to personal bondage and servitude, so vividly depicted in Socialism and Bureaucracy. There can be no compromise between these and the Brotherhood who are fighting for freedom for the human race, for their self-reliance, their independent thinking, their individual liberty and happiness, and the spread of love and good will everywhere, for that higher evolution and that freedom without which true Brotherhood amongst men could not survive. To compromise with such would at once destroy the very fundamental principles upon which Freemasonry was founded.

Against such it is our duty to fight, to destroy

their very existence as pestilent evils to humanity; there cannot be any association between the two; it would be as incomprehensible and incompatible as the blending of good spirits with evil ones.

That is the reason why the Masons of Germany and other countries we have been fighting against should never be admitted into our Lodges or Brotherhood again. They have betrayed their trusts and obligations, and if they have not actually assisted in all the horrors that so many poor humans have suffered, they have at least upheld and supported those whose actions have been a thousandfold worse than those of the most degraded savages in past ages. Therefore, to admit and associate with any such as these would reduce all those great principles which we have inherited direct from T.G.A.O.T.U. in past ages, and which we profess to believe and practise, to a farce. There could be no Universal Brotherhood, because there would be elements antagonistic and false in the combination—false to its principles, false to its morality and false to their God—and in the end it would, as a whole, become destroyed again, and the remnants would be scattered over the face of earth and water with only a survival of the few, as it has been before.

No, Brothers; we must be true to our obligations, true to our principles of morality, true to all our tenets, and ever fight against those evils which impose tyranny, thraldom of body or mind, and oppression in every form.

Thus acting, we can assist as His servants and instruments in raising the poor human to a happier and higher state of evolution, and once more become the great governing body throughout the world for this end as of old, for 300,000 years, before Socialism and Bureaucracy destroyed it.

The ethics of Freemasonry teach the gnosis to obtain the everlasting Spiritual Life, which ethics were first promulgated by Taht Aan in *The Ritual of Resurrection of the Egyptian Book of Life*, and these have been carried down through the past ages of time by the so-called Speculative Freemasons, time and circumstances being the causes of substituting the innovations in place of those fragments which have been lost, or as yet have not been found; and the inability of the compilers of our present *Ritual* to understand the Hieroglyphic and Sign Language in which the *Ritual* is written. That *Ritual of the Resurrection and the Life to Come* still stands good to-day, as it did 300,000 years ago or more.

INDEX

INDEX

Order From Your Favorite Bookseller Or Call For Our Free Catalog

Of Heaven and Earth: Essays Presented at the First Sitchin Studies Day, edited by Zecharia Sitchin. ISBN 1-885395-17-5 • 164 pages • 5 1/2 x 8 1/2 • trade paper • illustrated • $14.95

God Games: What Do You Do Forever?, by Neil Freer. ISBN 1-885395-39-6 • 312 pages • 6 x 9 • trade paper • $19.95

Space Travelers and the Genesis of the Human Form: Evidence of Intelligent Contact in the Solar System, by Joan d'Arc. ISBN 1-58509-127-8 • 208 pages • 6 x 9 • trade paper • illustrated • $18.95

Humanity's Extraterrestrial Origins: ET Influences on Humankind's Biological and Cultural Evolution, by Dr. Arthur David Horn with Lynette Mallory-Horn. ISBN 3-931652-31-9 • 373 pages • 6 x 9 • trade paper • $17.00

Past Shock: The Origin of Religion and Its Impact on the Human Soul, by Jack Barranger. ISBN 1-885395-08-6 • 126 pages • 6 x 9 • trade paper • illustrated • $12.95

Flying Serpents and Dragons: The Story of Mankind's Reptilian Past, by R.A. Boulay. ISBN 1-885395-38-8 • 276 pages • 6 x 9 • trade paper • illustrated • $19.95

Triumph of the Human Spirit: The Greatest Achievements of the Human Soul and How Its Power Can Change Your Life, by Paul Tice. ISBN 1-885395-57-4 • 295 pages • 6 x 9 • trade paper • illustrated • $19.95

Mysteries Explored: The Search for Human Origins, UFOs, and Religious Beginnings, by Jack Barranger and Paul Tice. ISBN 1-58509-101-4 • 104 pages • 6 x 9 • trade paper • $12.95

Mushrooms and Mankind: The Impact of Mushrooms on Human Consciousness and Religion, by James Arthur. ISBN 1-58509-151-0 • 180 pages • 6 x 9 • trade paper • $16.95

Vril or Vital Magnetism, with an Introduction by Paul Tice. ISBN 1-58509-030-1 • 124 pages • 5 1/2 x 8 1/2 • trade paper • $12.95

The Odic Force: Letters on Od and Magnetism, by Karl von Reichenbach. ISBN 1-58509-001-8 • 192 pages • 6 x 9 • trade paper • $15.95

The New Revelation: The Coming of a New Spiritual Paradigm, by Arthur Conan Doyle. ISBN 1-58509-220-7 • 124 pages • 6 x 9 • trade paper • $12.95

The Astral World: Its Scenes, Dwellers, and Phenomena, by Swami Panchadasi. ISBN 1-58509-071-9 • 104 pages • 6 x 9 • trade paper • $11.95

Reason and Belief: The Impact of Scientific Discovery on Religious and Spiritual Faith, by Sir Oliver Lodge. ISBN 1-58509-226-6 • 180 pages • 6 x 9 • trade paper • $17.95

William Blake: A Biography, by Basil De Selincourt. ISBN 1-58509-225-8 • 384 pages • 6 x 9 • trade paper • $28.95

The Divine Pymander: And Other Writings of Hermes Trismegistus, translated by John D. Chambers. ISBN 1-58509-046-8 • 196 pages • 6 x 9 • trade paper • $16.95

Theosophy and The Secret Doctrine, by Harriet L. Henderson. Includes ***H.P. Blavatsky: An Outline of Her Life,*** by Herbert Whyte, ISBN 1-58509-075-1 • 132 pages • 6 x 9 • trade paper • $13.95

The Light of Egypt, Volume One: The Science of the Soul and the Stars, by Thomas H. Burgoyne. ISBN 1-58509-051-4 • 320 pages • 6 x 9 • trade paper • illustrated • $24.95

The Light of Egypt, Volume Two: The Science of the Soul and the Stars, by Thomas H. Burgoyne. ISBN 1-58509-052-2 • 224 pages • 6 x 9 • trade paper • illustrated • $17.95

The Jumping Frog and 18 Other Stories: 19 Unforgettable Mark Twain Stories, by Mark Twain. ISBN 1-58509-200-2 • 128 pages • 6 x 9 • trade paper • $12.95

The Devil's Dictionary: A Guidebook for Cynics, by Ambrose Bierce. ISBN 1-58509-016-6 • 144 pages • 6 x 9 • trade paper • $12.95

The Smoky God: Or The Voyage to the Inner World, by Willis George Emerson. ISBN 1-58509-067-0 • 184 pages • 6 x 9 • trade paper • illustrated • $15.95

A Short History of the World, by H.G. Wells. ISBN 1-58509-211-8 • 320 pages • 6 x 9 • trade paper • $24.95

The Voyages and Discoveries of the Companions of Columbus, by Washington Irving. ISBN 1-58509-500-1 • 352 pages • 6 x 9 • hard cover • $39.95

History of Baalbek, by Michel Alouf. ISBN 1-58509-063-8 • 196 pages • 5 x 8 • trade paper • illustrated • $15.95

Ancient Egyptian Masonry: The Building Craft, by Sommers Clarke and R. Engelback. ISBN 1-58509-059-X • 350 pages • 6 x 9 • trade paper • illustrated • $26.95

That Old Time Religion: The Story of Religious Foundations, by Jordan Maxwell and Paul Tice. ISBN 1-58509-100-6 • 220 pages • 6 x 9 • trade paper • $19.95

Jumpin' Jehovah: Exposing the Atrocities of the Old Testament God, by Paul Tice. ISBN 1-58509-102-2 • 104 pages • 6 x 9 • trade paper • $12.95

The Book of Enoch: A Work of Visionary Revelation and Prophecy, Revealing Divine Secrets and Fantastic Information about Creation, Salvation, Heaven and Hell, translated by R. H. Charles. ISBN 1-58509-019-0 • 152 pages • 5 1/2 x 8 1/2 • trade paper • $13.95

The Book of Enoch: Translated from the Editor's Ethiopic Text and Edited with an Enlarged Introduction, Notes and Indexes, Together with a Reprint of the Greek Fragments, edited by R. H. Charles. ISBN 1-58509-080-8 • 448 pages • 6 x 9 • trade paper • $34.95

The Book of the Secrets of Enoch, translated from the Slavonic by W. R. Morfill. Edited, with Introduction and Notes by R. H. Charles. ISBN 1-58509-020-4 • 148 pages • 5 1/2 x 8 1/2 • trade paper • $13.95

Enuma Elish: The Seven Tablets of Creation, Volume One, by L. W. King. ISBN 1-58509-041-7 • 236 pages • 6 x 9 • trade paper • illustrated • $18.95

Enuma Elish: The Seven Tablets of Creation, Volume Two, by L. W. King. ISBN 1-58509-042-5 • 260 pages • 6 x 9 • trade paper • illustrated • $19.95

Enuma Elish, Volumes One and Two: The Seven Tablets of Creation, by L. W. King. Two volumes from above bound as one. ISBN 1-58509-043-3 • 496 pages • 6 x 9 • trade paper • illustrated • $38.90

The Archko Volume: Documents that Claim Proof to the Life, Death, and Resurrection of Christ, by Drs. McIntosh and Twyman. ISBN 1-58509-082-4 • 248 pages • 6 x 9 • trade paper • $20.95

The Lost Language of Symbolism: An Inquiry into the Origin of Certain Letters, Words, Names, Fairy-Tales, Folklore, and Mythologies, by Harold Bayley. ISBN 1-58509-070-0 • 384 pages • 6 x 9 • trade paper • $27.95

The Book of Jasher: A Suppressed Book that was Removed from the Bible, Referred to in Joshua and Second Samuel, translated by Albinus Alcuin (800 AD). ISBN 1-58509-081-6 • 304 pages • 6 x 9 • trade paper • $24.95

The Bible's Most Embarrassing Moments, with an Introduction by Paul Tice. ISBN 1-58509-025-5 • 172 pages • 5 x 8 • trade paper • $14.95

History of the Cross: The Pagan Origin and Idolatrous Adoption and Worship of the Image, by Henry Dana Ward. ISBN 1-58509-056-5 • 104 pages • 6 x 9 • trade paper • illustrated • $11.95

Was Jesus Influenced by Buddhism? A Comparative Study of the Lives and Thoughts of Gautama and Jesus, by Dwight Goddard. ISBN 1-58509-027-1 • 252 pages • 6 x 9 • trade paper • $19.95

History of the Christian Religion to the Year Two Hundred, by Charles B. Waite. ISBN 1-885395-15-9 • 556 pages. • 6 x 9 • hard cover • $25.00

Symbols, Sex, and the Stars, by Ernest Busenbark. ISBN 1-885395-19-1 • 396 pages • 5 1/2 x 8 1/2 • trade paper • $22.95

History of the First Council of Nice: A World's Christian Convention, A.D. 325, by Dean Dudley. ISBN 1-58509-023-9 • 132 pages • 5 1/2 x 8 1/2 • trade paper • $12.95

The World's Sixteen Crucified Saviors, by Kersey Graves. ISBN 1-58509-018-2 • 436 pages • 5 1/2 x 8 1/2 • trade paper • $29.95

ORDER FROM YOUR FAVORITE BOOKSELLER OR CALL FOR OUR FREE CATALOG

Babylonian Influence on the Bible and Popular Beliefs: A Comparative Study of Genesis I.2, by A. Smythe Palmer. ISBN 1-58509-000-X • 124 pages • 6 x 9 • trade paper • $12.95

Biography of Satan: Exposing the Origins of the Devil, by Kersey Graves. ISBN 1-885395-11-6 • 168 pages • 5 1/2 x 8 1/2 • trade paper • $13.95

The Malleus Maleficarum: The Notorious Handbook Once Used to Condemn and Punish "Witches", by Heinrich Kramer and James Sprenger. ISBN 1-58509-098-0 • 332 pages • 6 x 9 • trade paper • $25.95

Crux Ansata: An Indictment of the Roman Catholic Church, by H. G. Wells. ISBN 1-58509-210-X • 160 pages • 6 x 9 • trade paper • $14.95

Emanuel Swedenborg: The Spiritual Columbus, by U.S.E. (William Spear). ISBN 1-58509-096-4 • 208 pages • 6 x 9 • trade paper • $17.95

Dragons and Dragon Lore, by Ernest Ingersoll. ISBN 1-58509-021-2 • 228 pages • 6 x 9 • trade paper • illustrated • $17.95

The Vision of God, by Nicholas of Cusa. ISBN 1-58509-004-2 • 160 pages • 5 x 8 • trade paper • $13.95

The Historical Jesus and the Mythical Christ: Separating Fact From Fiction, by Gerald Massey. ISBN 1-58509-073-5 • 244 pages • 6 x 9 • trade paper • $18.95

Gog and Magog: The Giants in Guildhall; Their Real and Legendary History, with an Account of Other Giants at Home and Abroad, by F.W. Fairholt. ISBN 1-58509-084-0 • 172 pages • 6 x 9 • trade paper • $16.95

The Origin and Evolution of Religion, by Albert Churchward. ISBN 1-58509-078-6 • 504 pages • 6 x 9 • trade paper • $39.95

The Origin of Biblical Traditions, by Albert T. Clay. ISBN 1-58509-065-4 • 220 pages • 5 1/2 x 8 1/2 • trade paper • $17.95

Aryan Sun Myths, by Sarah Elizabeth Titcomb, Introduction by Charles Morris. ISBN 1-58509-069-7 • 192 pages • 6 x 9 • trade paper • $15.95

The Social Record of Christianity, by Joseph McCabe. Includes ***The Lies and Fallacies of the Encyclopedia Britannica,*** ISBN 1-58509-215-0 • 204 pages • 6 x 9 • trade paper • $17.95

The History of the Christian Religion and Church During the First Three Centuries, by Dr. Augustus Neander. ISBN 1-58509-077-8 • 112 pages • 6 x 9 • trade paper • $12.95

Ancient Symbol Worship: Influence of the Phallic Idea in the Religions of Antiquity, by Hodder M. Westropp and C. Staniland Wake. ISBN 1-58509-048-4 • 120 pages • 6 x 9 • trade paper • illustrated • $12.95

The Gnosis: Or Ancient Wisdom in the Christian Scriptures, by William Kingsland. ISBN 1-58509-047-6 • 232 pages • 6 x 9 • trade paper • $18.95

The Evolution of the Idea of God: An Inquiry into the Origin of Religions, by Grant Allen. ISBN 1-58509-074-3 • 160 pages • 6 x 9 • trade paper • $14.95

Sun Lore of All Ages: A Survey of Solar Mythology, Folklore, Customs, Worship, Festivals, and Superstition, by William Tyler Olcott. ISBN 1-58509-044-1 • 316 pages • 6 x 9 • trade paper • $24.95

Nature Worship: An Account of Phallic Faiths and Practices Ancient and Modern, by the Author of Phallicism with an Introduction by Tedd St. Rain. ISBN 1-58509-049-2 • 112 pages • 6 x 9 • trade paper • illustrated • $12.95

Life and Religion, by Max Muller. ISBN 1-885395-10-8 • 237 pages • 5 1/2 x 8 1/2 • trade paper • $14.95

Jesus: God, Man, or Myth? An Examination of the Evidence, by Herbert Cutner. ISBN 1-58509-072-7 • 304 pages • 6 x 9 • trade paper • $23.95

Pagan and Christian Creeds: Their Origin and Meaning, by Edward Carpenter. ISBN 1-58509-024-7 • 316 pages • 5 1/2 x 8 1/2 • trade paper • $24.95

The Christ Myth: A Study, by Elizabeth Evans. ISBN 1-58509-037-9 • 136 pages • 6 x 9 • trade paper • $13.95

Popery: Foe of the Church and the Republic, by Joseph F. Van Dyke. ISBN 1-58509-058-1 • 336 pages • 6 x 9 • trade paper • illustrated • $25.95

Career of Religious Ideas, by Hudson Tuttle. ISBN 1-58509-066-2 • 172 pages • 5 x 8 • trade paper • $15.95

Buddhist Suttas: Major Scriptural Writings from Early Buddhism, by T.W. Rhys Davids. ISBN 1-58509-079-4 • 376 pages • 6 x 9 • trade paper • $27.95

Early Buddhism, by T. W. Rhys Davids. Includes ***Buddhist Ethics: The Way to Salvation?,*** by Paul Tice. ISBN 1-58509-076-X • 112 pages • 6 x 9 • trade paper • $12.95

The Fountain-Head of Religion: A Comparative Study of the Principal Religions of the World and a Manifestation of their Common Origin from the Vedas, by Ganga Prasad. ISBN 1-58509-054-9 • 276 pages • 6 x 9 • trade paper • $22.95

India: What Can It Teach Us?, by Max Muller. ISBN 1-58509-064-6 • 284 pages • 5 1/2 x 8 1/2 • trade paper • $22.95

Matrix of Power: How the World has Been Controlled by Powerful People Without Your Knowledge, by Jordan Maxwell. ISBN 1-58509-120-0 • 104 pages • 6 x 9 • trade paper • $12.95

Cyberculture Counterconspiracy: A Steamshovel Web Reader, Volume One, edited by Kenn Thomas. ISBN 1-58509-125-1 • 180 pages • 6 x 9 • trade paper • illustrated • $16.95

Cyberculture Counterconspiracy: A Steamshovel Web Reader, Volume Two, edited by Kenn Thomas. ISBN 1-58509-126-X • 132 pages • 6 x 9 • trade paper • illustrated • $13.95

Oklahoma City Bombing: The Suppressed Truth, by Jon Rappoport. ISBN 1-885395-22-1 • 112 pages • 5 1/2 x 8 1/2 • trade paper • $12.95

The Protocols of the Learned Elders of Zion, by Victor Marsden. ISBN 1-58509-015-8 • 312 pages • 6 x 9 • trade paper • $24.95

Secret Societies and Subversive Movements, by Nesta H. Webster. ISBN 1-58509-092-1 • 432 pages • 6 x 9 • trade paper • $29.95

The Secret Doctrine of the Rosicrucians, by Magus Incognito. ISBN 1-58509-091-3 • 256 pages • 6 x 9 • trade paper • $20.95

The Origin and Evolution of Freemasonry: Connected with the Origin and Evolution of the Human Race, by Albert Churchward. ISBN 1-58509-029-8 • 240 pages • 6 x 9 • trade paper • $18.95

The Lost Key: An Explanation and Application of Masonic Symbols, by Prentiss Tucker. ISBN 1-58509-050-6 • 192 pages • 6 x 9 • trade paper • illustrated • $15.95

The Character, Claims, and Practical Workings of Freemasonry, by Rev. C.G. Finney. ISBN 1-58509-094-8 • 288 pages • 6 x 9 • trade paper • $22.95

The Secret World Government or "The Hidden Hand": The Unrevealed in History, by Maj.-Gen., Count Cherep-Spiridovich. ISBN 1-58509-093-X • 270 pages • 6 x 9 • trade paper • $21.95

The Magus, Book One: A Complete System of Occult Philosophy, by Francis Barrett. ISBN 1-58509-031-X • 200 pages • 6 x 9 • trade paper • illustrated • $16.95

The Magus, Book Two: A Complete System of Occult Philosophy, by Francis Barrett. ISBN 1-58509-032-8 • 220 pages • 6 x 9 • trade paper • illustrated • $17.95

The Magus, Book One and Two: A Complete System of Occult Philosophy, by Francis Barrett. ISBN 1-58509-033-6 • 420 pages • 6 x 9 • trade paper • illustrated • $34.90

The Key of Solomon The King, by S. Liddell MacGregor Mathers. ISBN 1-58509-022-0 • 152 pages • 6 x 9 • trade paper • illustrated • $12.95

Magic and Mystery in Tibet, by Alexandra David-Neel. ISBN 1-58509-097-2 • 352 pages • 6 x 9 • trade paper • $26.95

The Comte de St. Germain, by I. Cooper Oakley. ISBN 1-58509-068-9 • 280 pages • 6 x 9 • trade paper • illustrated • $22.95

Alchemy Rediscovered and Restored, by A. Cockren. ISBN 1-58509-028-X • 156 pages • 5 1/2 x 8 1/2 • trade paper • $13.95

The 6th and 7th Books of Moses, with an Introduction by Paul Tice. ISBN 1-58509-045-X • 188 pages • 6 x 9 • trade paper • illustrated • $16.95

www.ingramcontent.com/pod-product-compliance
Lightning Source LLC
Chambersburg PA
CBHW021542260326
41914CB00001B/125
* 9 7 8 1 5 8 5 0 9 5 7 1 1 *